for the
INTERNATIONAL BACCALAUREATE

Business Management Workbook

For use with Business Management 4th Edition

Paul Hoang

www.ibid.com.au

First published in 2018 by IBID Press, Victoria, Australia.

Library Catalogue:

Hoang P.

1. Business Management Workbook 3rd Edition

2. International Baccalaureate.

Series Title: International Baccalaureate in Detail

ISBN: 978-1-921917-95-0

IBID Press express their thanks to the International Baccalaureate Organization for permission to reproduce its intellectual property.

Published by IBID Press, 36 Quail Crescent, Melton, 3337, Australia.

Cover design by Key-Strokes.

Printed by KHL Printing Co Pte Ltd

Dedication

Dedicated to my students at Sha Tin College,

English Schools Foundation, Hong Kong

Message from the author

Dear students (and teachers),

I hope that you find this Workbook to be of value in preparing you for reviewing your learning of IB Business Management.

There are several ways that you can use the Workbook:

- To review the units that you have studied with your teachers in class
- As end of topic tests (set by your teachers or as part of your self-assessment) during the two year IB Diploma course
- As a revision tool prior to the final examinations

The solutions to all the questions are available on the IBID Press website to aid your revision and learning. However, please be disciplined and refrain from looking at the answers before you have attempted the questions (making mistakes is an essential part of the learning process!) The Workbook supplements the main textbook *Business Management, for use with the IB Diploma Programme*, now in its 4th edition, also published by IBID Press.

Finally, please allow me the opportunity to wish you the very best for your forthcoming IB examinations.

Paul Hoang

E: paulhoang88@gmail.com

T: @paulhoang88

About This Book

This fully revised Workbook is intended for use by students following the International Baccalaureate course in Business Management (first exams 2016) and accompanies the main textbook *Business Management, for use with the IB Diploma Programme*, now in its fourth edition available from IBID Press.

The Workbook can be used as end-of-topic reviews throughout the two-year course or it can simply be used as a revision tool prior to the examinations. There are cloze 'fill-in-the-blank' tasks, key terms and concepts quizzes, short-answer examination-style questions and 855 multiple choice questions.

For teachers, the Workbook can help to reduce their lesson planning time. The tasks can also be used to promote independent learning in and out of the classroom. The accompanying Solutions Guide to the Workbook can be used for self, peer or teacher marking.

Paul Hoang teaches at Sha Tin College, English Schools Foundation in Hong Kong where he is Vice Principal. He has experience as an examiner and paper setter, and has been an IB Workshop Leader for over 10 years. Paul is also author of the best-selling textbook for the course, *Business Management, for use with the IB Diploma Programme*, also published by IBID Press.

ISBN 978-1-921917-90-5 Business Management 4th Edition

Contents

Unit 1.1 Introduction to business management

Task 1: Complete the missing words

A business is a decision-making organization that uses inputs, known as the factors of production to produce goods and services. The four factors of production are land, labour, __________, __________. Products are physical products, such as pens, televisions and clothing. Services are intangible products such as education, health care and foreign holidays.

Production is the process of using factors of production to generate the __________ of goods and services. These are then purchased by customers (the people or businesses that *buy* the product) and then used by consumers (the end users, whether they are businesses or individuals).

A business __________ is used as a management tool to report how an organization intends to achieve its goals and objectives. It requires managers to consider the use of marketing, finance and human resources in order to meet these aims and objectives.

Task 2: Vocabulary quiz

a. Identify the correct stage of production from the clues below.

Stage of production	Description
Primary	Extraction of natural resources such as farming and mining.
Quarternary	Involved in intellectual, knowledge-based activities that generate and share information, e.g. R&D.
Secondary	Transforms primary resources into manufactured goods for sale.
Tertiary	The provision of services such as distribution and after-sales care.

b. Find the correct factor of production from the given definitions.

Factor of production	Definition
	The non-natural (manufactured) resources used to further the production process, e.g. buildings, machinery, tools and vehicles.
	An individual who has the skills and ability to take risks in organizing the other factors of production to generate output in a profitable way.
Labour	The physical human effort and psychological intellect used in the production process.
land	All natural resources that are used in the production process, e.g. wood, water, physical land and minerals.
entrapreneur	The act of being an entrepreneur but as an employee within a large business.

c. Identify the correct functional department in each case below.

Functional department	Functional roles
Finance + accounts	Prepares the final accounts such as profit and loss accounts, cash flow statements and balance sheets; manages the money of the business.
HR	Handles recruitment, training, appraisal and the general welfare (well-being) of the workforce.
Marketing	Conducts research to meet the needs of customers; arranges promotional activities to sell the firm's products.
Operations	Manufactures goods in order to meet quality standards, targets and deadlines.

Task 3: Explain …

a. Two differences between intrapreneurship and entrepreneurship.

b. Three qualities of successful entrepreneurs.

- risk takers
- innovative

c. Two reasons why people set up their own businesses.

- New idea for product or Service
- Want greater control over business

d. Two problems that new businesses are likely to face.

- acquiring funds
- lack of management experience

Task 4: Multiple choice

1. What are the resources used in the production process collectively known as?

A. Capital resources

B. Factors of production

C. Raw materials

D. Working capital

2. Consumers are the people or businesses that

A. Buy and use goods and services

B. Buy goods and services

C. Pay for a good or service without using it

D. Use a good or service

3. Which of the following is not an example of primary production?

   A. Agriculture

   B. Coaching

   C. Fishing

   D. Mining

4. Which of the following is not classed as land as a factor of production?

   A. Coal

   B. Fish

   C. Paper

   D. Water

5. The difference between the cost of the inputs in the production process and the final price of the output is known as

   A. Income

   B. Profit

   C. Revenue

   D. Value added

6. The primary sector is the part of the economy that consists of

   A. Agriculture, fishing and extractive industries

   B. Businesses that have been recently set up

   C. Organizations that provide value-added services to their customers

   D. Organizations that use extracted raw materials for production

7. An entrepreneur is someone who

   A. Has a managerial or supervisory role within an organization

   B. Is an business person who manages production and output

   C. Organizes factors of production and takes the risks of decision-making

   D. Owns a business as a sole trader or as the primary owner

8. Production is

   A. Any output other than services

   B. The manufacturing of goods in the secondary industry

   C. The process of making products from the available resources

   D. The second stage of the output process

9. The term 'product' refers to

   A. Both goods and services

   B. Goods only

   C. Services only

   D. The physical attributes of a good

10. The __________ sector of the economy is owned by individuals and companies, usually in pursuit of making profit. The __________ sector is controlled by the government and aims primarily to provide a service by acting in the public's best interest.

    A. Primary, Tertiary

    B. Private, Public

    C. Public, Private

    D. Tertiary, Primary

11. Which of the occupations below does not exist in the tertiary sector?

    A. Librarian

    B. Machinist

    C. Real estate agent

    D. Secretary

12. The secondary sector

    A. Consists of businesses involved in the manufacturing of physical goods

    B. Forms the largest employment sector in most high income countries

    C. Provides both goods and services

    D. Tends to be labour intensive

13. Which of the following does not apply to the quaternary industry?

    A. A sub-category of the tertiary sector

    B. Capital intensity

    C. Development of expertise and skills

    D. Improved efficiency of production

14. Which of the following businesses does not operate in the tertiary sector?

    A. Pest control

    B. Restaurants

    C. Private security firms

    D. Textiles

15. The process of increasing the value of a resource in the production process is known as

A. Adding value

B. Production process

C. Sectoral change

D. The chain of production

16. Computer systems are an example of which type of factor input?

A. Capital

B. Intrapreneurship

C. Land

D. Labour

17. Which of the following statements is correct?

A. Automation has caused a decline in the secondary sector in many countries

B. Manufacturing accounts for the largest value-added sector of an economy

C. The primary sector is the largest part of the economy in most high income countries

D. The quaternary sector accounts for the largest sector of employment in most countries

18. Public utilities, such as water and gas supply, are usually considered as being in the tertiary sector because they

A. Are involved with turning resources into a useable product

B. Are not extracted or manufactured

C. Are owned by the government

D. Provide services to the general public

19. Which of the following would not be regarded as part of the tertiary sector?

A. Education and training

B. Engineering

C. Insurance

D. Leisure and tourism

20. Which of the following does not apply to most business start-ups?

A. Business registration documentation is required prior to trading

B. It requires a business plan to minimise risks

C. It requires intrapreneurial skills

D. Owners of the business have to obtain finance

Unit 1.2 Types of organizations

Task 1: Complete the missing words

A sole trader is a business owned and run by a single person. Such firms are very common, partly because there are few legal procedures involved in setting up the business. The owner bears all the responsibility of running the business but has full control, and gets to reap all profit that the business earns. However, the owner also has unlimited liability, meaning that he or she may need to sell personal possessions in order to pay off any debts that the business may have.

An ordinary partnership is an alliance of between 2 and 20 individual owners who are jointly responsible for the affairs of the business (although the maximum number can vary in different countries). The joint owners will usually sign a mutually agreed contract known as the __________ ____ ______________. Most, if not all, of the partners face unlimited liability for any debts they might incur. Partners that simply place their money into the business as an investment and without any direct involvement in the business are known as silent partners. These partners enjoy limited liability.

cooperatives are for-profit social enterprises owned and run by their members (usually employees or customers). Their primary aim is to create value for their members by being socially responsible. They share any profits earned between their board?.

Non-profit social enterprises are businesses run in a commercial-like manner but without profit being the main goal. For example, non-prof. org. (NPOs) use their surplus revenues to achieve their social goals, rather than distributing the surplus as profits or dividends to shareholders. A non-gov't. org (NGO) is a non-profit social enterprise that operates in the private sector of the economy, i.e. it is not owned or controlled by the government. However, NGOs do not aim primarily to make a profit.

Companies are owned by ______________, who have limited liability. This is because all limited liability companies are ______________ businesses, i.e. the organizations are treated as separate legal entities from their owners. Shareholders get one __________ for each share that they own in the company. Private limited companies tend to be relatively small companies that are owned by family members. In order to become a public limited company, the firm has to sell shares to the public for the first time, known as an Initial public offering (IPO). In return for their investment, shareholders are given a proportion of the company's profits (if any is earned) in the form of dividend payments, which are usually paid once a year. The declared payment is paid on each share that a shareholder owns, so the more shares held the higher the total payout will be. Shareholders also buy shares in the hope that there is a ______________ gain, i.e. the share price rises.

Task 2: Vocabulary quiz

Identify the key terms from the clues given. *Hint*: the answers are in alphabetical order.

Key term	Definition
	These altruistic businesses operate predominantly in the private sector with the objectives of promoting a socially worthwhile cause..
cooperatives	For-profit social enterprises owned and run by their members, such as employees or customers, striving to create value for their members.
IPO	Term used to describe a private limited company offering its shares on the stock exchange for the first time, thereby changing its legal status to a public limited company
microfinance providers	Organizations that grant finance to entrepreneurs of small businesses, especially females and those on low incomes.
non-profit org.	Private sector businesses that do not primarily aim to make a profit for their owners.
	Organizations established by the government and one or more private sector organizations to jointly provide certain goods or services.

Key term	Definition
	Businesses in this sector are run and owned by the government in order to provide communal services for society, e.g. state education and health care.
Silent partner	An investor in a partnership that does not get involved in the day to day management of the business.
	Organizations that are revenue-generating businesses with community (general public) objectives at the core of their operations.
	This is the marketplace for buying and selling second-hand company stocks and shares.
unlimited liability	Refers to the limitless amount of debt that the owner(s) of a sole trader or partnership business can incur if things do not go well.

Task 3: True or false?

		True/False
a.	A not-for-profit organization is any business that does not primarily aim to make a profit.	T
b.	A public limited company can advertise its shares and have them quoted on a stock exchange.	T
c.	A stock exchange represents the market where secondhand shares can be bought and sold.	T
d.	All non-governmental organizations (NGOs) operate in the private sector.	F
e.	*Limited liability* means that if a firm is unable to pay back its debts, the owners of the business can lose everything, including their personal possessions.	F
f.	Microfinance providers are an example of social enterprises.	T
g.	Public companies are examples of private sector businesses.	F
h.	Social enterprises do not strive to make a profit. There are for-profit social enterprises that exist (e.g. cooperatives and microfinance providers).	
i.	State-owned enterprises are also known as public companies.	
j.	The liability of shareholders is limited to the amount of their investment.	T

Task 4: Explain one …

a. Benefit of a business staying small.

Greater control over business processes and decisions.

b. Purpose of holding an Annual General Meeting (AGM).

c. Feature of the private sector.

Always have a way to aqcuire funds by initiating an IPO

d. Feature of charities.

____

____

e. Difference between a state-owned enterprise and a public company.

____

____

f. Advantage of being a private limited company.

____

____

Task 5: Multiple choice

1. Which statement does not apply to sole traders?

A. A business that is owned by one person

B. The most common form of business ownership

C. There can be more than one employer

D. There may be more than one employee

2. A sole trader is a person who

A. Forms a business with another person

B. Has exclusive responsibility for the running of the business

C. Is not legally liable for any debts of the business

D. Sets up the safest form of business organization

3. In comparison to other forms of business, sole proprietors face the problem of

A. Administration and set-up procedures

B. Continuity

C. Privacy of financial accounts

D. Specialisation

4. Disadvantages of sole traders do not include

A. A reliance on the efforts and liability of just one person

B. Autonomy in decision making

C. Constraint of lack of time and specialisation to complete all tasks

D. The demands of having to be multi-skilled

5. Advantages of sole traders do not include

A. A high degree of confidentiality in administration and financial reporting

B. Flexibility and freedom in decision-making

C. Profits not having to be shared with others

D. The various sources of finance available

6. Which of the following is not a reason why people may choose to set up their own business?

A. There is a lack of employment opportunities

B. There are higher risks than working for someone else

C. To enjoy autonomy in decision-making

D. To extend personal interests and hobbies

7. Which of the following is not a necessary condition for an ordinary partnership?

A. Having at least one partner with unlimited liability

B. Having between 2 to 20 partners

C. Shares cannot be issued by the business

D. Signing the contents of a partnership deed This is a recommendation only, rather than a formal requirement

8. Which of the following is least likely to be a disadvantage of a partnership?

A. Having less control of business activities

B. Having to share profits with other partners

C. Managing conflict and disagreements

D. Spreading workload with other partners

9. The legal document that sets out the constitution of a limited liability company is known as the

A. Articles of Association

B. Certificate of Incorporation

C. Deed of Incorporation

D. Memorandum of Association

10. Which document is issued to a limited liability company before it can start trading?

A. Articles of Association

B. Certificate of Incorporation

C. Deed of Partnership

D. Memorandum of Association

11. A Memorandum of Association

   A. Sets out rules for the appointment and remuneration of directors

   B. Shows how profits will be distributed to its owners

   C. States the main purpose of a limited liability company

   D. Stipulates the internal functions and rules of an organization

12. Which of these statements is false?

   A. A private limited company cannot sell its shares on a stock exchange

   B. Public limited companies operate in the private sector

   C. Second-hand shares of public companies can be traded on a stock exchange

   D. The Board of Directors of a private limited company own the business

13. Which of the statements about shareholders is correct?

   A. An advantage for shareholders is having limited liability

   B. As co-owners of a company, shareholders have equal voting rights

   C. Shareholders are paid annual dividends for investing in the company

   D. They own and control private and public limited companies

14. Identify the incorrect statement below.

   A. A Deed of Partnership is advised for ordinary partnerships as it helps to resolve disagreements

   B. A silent partner is another name for a sleeping partner

   C. Public companies operate in the public sector

   D. Shareholders are not personally liable for the debts of the company

15. The shareholders of a company

   A. Are legally entitled to a share of any profits earned

   B. Are wealthier than sole traders or partners

   C. Control the running of the business

   D. Earn a capital gain in their investment by selling their shares

16. 'Unincorporated' means that a business

   A. Has shareholders

   B. Has unlimited liability for its debts

   C. Is a separate legal entity from its owners

   D. Is protected by limited liability

17. A drawback of public limited companies is that they

A. Have limited liability

B. Have to publish certain financial information to all stakeholders

C. Rely on government funding

D. Represent high risks to investors

18. What is the other name for a Public Limited Company?

A. Joint stock company

B. Limited liability company

C. Private sector company

D. Privately held company

19. A public–private enterprise is set up in order to

A. Earn profits as a social enterprise

B. Privatise the provision of certain services such as schools and hospitals

C. Reduce the risks of share ownership

D. Replace the government in the provision of goods and services to the general public

20. A public sector enterprise is

A. An organization owned by private shareholders only

B. An organization owned by shareholders who can trade their shares on a stock exchange

C. An organization owned by the state or government

D. Any business that carries 'PLC' after its name

21. A non-profit organization that operates in the private sector and runs for the benefit of others in society is known as a

A. Charity

B. Non-governmental organization

C. Non-profit organization

D. Not-for-profit organization

22. Which of the following are for-profit organizations?

A. Charities

B. Cooperatives

C. Non-governmental organizations

D. State-owned enterprises

23. Which of the following is not classed as a social enterprise?

- **A.** Charities
- **B.** Consultancy service providers
- **C.** Microfinance providers
- **D.** Public-private partnerships

24. Which statement does not apply to charities?

- **A.** They are a type of not-for-profit organization
- **B.** They are private sector organizations
- **C.** They are registered as incorporated businesses
- **D.** They promote and raise money for good causes

25. Which of the following is *least* likely to be a non-profit organization?

- **A.** Museums
- **B.** Performing arts groups
- **C.** Police force
- **D.** Public transport firms

26. Microfinance providers

- **A.** Are a type of not-for-profit social enterprise
- **B.** Charge extremely high rates of interest to entrepreneurs who cannot use commercial banks
- **C.** Empower entrepreneurs of small businesses
- **D.** Grant financial support to female entrepreneurs only

27. Which of the following is an example of public (sector) expenditure?

- **A.** Donations made to charities and non-profit organizations
- **B.** Investment by public limited companies
- **C.** Spending by the general public on company stocks and shares
- **D.** Spending on state education and healthcare

28. Which of the following is not a non-profit social enterprise?

- **A.** Amnesty International
- **B.** Habitat for Humanity
- **C.** International Baccalaureate Organization (this is a NPO, but not a social enterprise)
- **D.** World Wide Fund for Nature

29. Charities get their finance from different sources. Which of these options is the exception?

A. Corporate tax refunds

B. Donations

C. Fund-raising events

D. Selling products

30. Which of these factors is *least* likely to affect the strategic choice of the most appropriate type of business organization?

A. The amount of finance needed

B. The products being sold

C. The size of the business and scale of its operations

D. Whether owners and investors want limited liability

Unit 1.3 Organizational objectives

Task 1: Complete the missing words

The ________ of a business are its long-term goals, which stem from the organization's ____________ statement. Hence, aims are a general statement of a firm's intentions, such as to become the market leader. They tend to be _______________ rather than quantitative in nature.

A business tends to find it difficult to satisfy all its stakeholders simultaneously due to their own ______________ objectives. For example, shareholders are likely to demand that the business aims for __________ maximisation, whilst employees will strive to maximise their own ___________ and benefits (thereby potentially reducing the profits of the business).

Organizations are increasingly concerned with the possible impact of their actions on the environment and society. This is largely because of the increased public awareness and concern for our planet's natural environment. Adverse business activity could lead to unwanted publicity from pressure groups. Such negative exposure can damage the ______________ of the business and reduce customer ______________. Unethical business practices might also adversely affect the firm's suppliers, employees, creditors and investors. Ultimately, ignoring ethics and social __________________ can seriously harm a firm's profitability. Hence, there are ever more driving forces pushing businesses to behave in a ________ responsible way.

SWOT analysis is a strategic planning that can help managers to reduce the _________ involved in decision-making. SWOT analysis involves exploring the current position of a product, department or the whole organization in terms of its ___________ and _____________, and to identify potential _____________ and ___________. It is also common to find a SWOT analysis within a _______________ plan.

Task 2: Match the terms

Read the definitions and match them with the correct business terms from the list below.

a.	Aims	**i.**	This declaration sets out the vision of an organization, to provide a shared purpose and direction for all stakeholders of the firm.
b.	Mission statement	**ii.**	This refers to the obligations that a business has towards its stakeholders and society as a whole.
c.	Objectives	**iii.**	The long-term goals of a business that provide direction for setting its objectives and targets.
d.	Social responsibility	**iv.**	The long-term actions a business takes in order to achieve its aims and objectives (what needs to be done, the resources needed to do it, and the timeframe in which to accomplish it).
e.	Strategy	**v.**	The (very) long-term desire or aspiration of an organization.
f.	Vision	**vi.**	These are the medium- to long-term goals and targets of an organization, e.g. survival, diversification and growth.

Task 3: Odd one out

Select the odd one out from each of the options below.

a.	Operational objectives	Secondary objectives	Strategic objectives	Tactical objectives
b.	Acquisition	Growth	Sales maximisation	Survival
c.	To control	To direct	To motivate	To select
d.	To become the world's market leader	To improve productive efficiency	To improve the quality of customer service	To reduce absenteeism and labour turnover

Task 4: True or false?

		True/False
a.	A business that adopts an ethical approach will tend to improve its profits in the long run.	
b.	All businesses have an aim to make profit for their owners.	
c.	All businesses in the private sector aim to make profit whereas those operating in the public sector aim primarily to provide a service to the general public.	
d.	Being socially responsible is the same as being environmentally responsible.	
e.	Ethical corporate responsibility considers the welfare of the workforce.	
f.	Examples of threats in a SWOT analysis include: price wars, oil crises, recession, natural disasters, and infectious diseases.	
g.	For most businesses, the objectives of shareholders are more important than those of other stakeholders.	
h.	If a business behaves ethically, its profits will fall in the short run.	
i.	Strategic objectives refer to the general organizational objectives of a business that encompass its long-term goals.	
j.	Survival is the main aim of businesses in the long term.	
k.	The growth strategy of selling new products in existing markets is called market development.	
l.	The overall purpose of an organization can often be seen from its mission statement.	

Task 5: Explain …

a. Why a business might choose to act unethically.

____

____

b. The purpose of producing an ethical code of practice in the workplace.

____

____

c. Why a business might choose to donate money to charitable organizations.

____

____

d. Whether polluting the environment is legal, illegal, and/or unethical in your country.

____

____

e. Why organizational objectives should be agreed through a process of consultation with employees rather than simply being set by senior managers.

f. Whether the following factors are strengths, weaknesses, opportunities or threats:

i. high gearing ratio.

ii. high market share.

iii. reduced entry barriers to the industry.

iv. new overseas markets to enter.

Task 6: Mission, vision or objective?

Choose from the following alternatives to complete the table below.

- Can be changed easily
- Core values and beliefs
- Motivational tool for employees
- Provides strategic direction for decision-making
- Purpose of the organization
- Source of inspiration
- Specific rather than idealistic
- Strategic planning tool
- Rarely reviewed
- Reviewed periodically
- The ideal image of the organization in the future
- What the company aspires to be

Vision	Mission	Objective

Task 7: The Ansoff matrix

a. Ansoff's matrix is a framework for devising growth strategies for a business. True or False?

b. Market penetration is the least risky strategy for business growth. True or False?

c. The highest risk strategy for growth is called ________________.

d. Skimming as a pricing strategy is most likely to feature in which of Ansoff's growth strategies?

____

e. Innovation and new ideas are features of which strategy for achieving growth?

____

f. According to Ansoff, aiming to increase market share would be a feature of which growth strategy?

____

g. Risk-bearing economies of scale can be enjoyed if a business pursues which growth strategy?

____

h. 'Buy One Get One Free' offers will help a business to increase its market share. True or False?

i. Complete the table below using the four growth strategies of Ansoff's matrix.

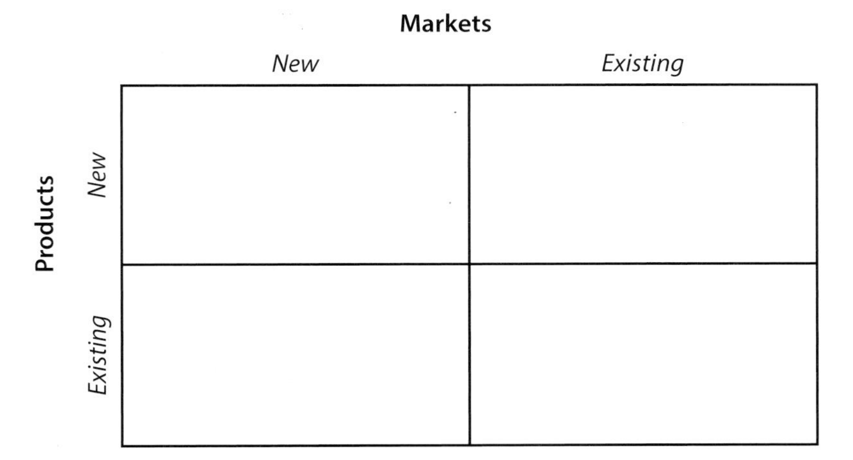

j. Explain why it is difficult to penetrate a saturated market.

____

____

k. Explain why diversification carries huge risks as a growth strategy.

____

____

Task 8: Multiple choice

1. Objectives are
   - **A.** Qualitative statements of a firm's strategic direction
   - **B.** The major goals of an organization
   - **C.** The purpose for a firm's existence
   - **D.** Qualitative statements of a firm's strategic direction

2. What is the term used to describe what an organization exists for and what it intends to achieve?
   - **A.** Business objectives
   - **B.** Business plan
   - **C.** Mission statement
   - **A.** Vision statement

3. Objectives of public sector organizations are least likely to include
   - **A.** To reach break-even as soon as possible
   - **B.** To maximise profitability
   - **C.** To provide a service to the community
   - **D.** To survive

4. The declaration of the future identity of a business is known as its
   - **A.** Business objectives
   - **B.** Corporate identity
   - **C.** Mission statement
   - **D.** Vision statement

5. Many businesses strive to be market leaders. Which of the following methods is least likely to achieve this objective?
   - **A.** Having a high labour turnover rate
   - **B.** Having a reputation for competitive prices
   - **C.** Maintaining customer satisfaction
   - **D.** Maintaining product quality

6. Objectives do not
   - **A.** Help to assess the performance of a business
   - **B.** Inform strategic planning
   - **C.** Provide a focus for the workforce
   - **D.** Suggest how goals should be achieved

7. Advantages of setting ethical objectives do not include

   A. A possible unique selling point for the firm

   B. An obligation to provide shareholder dividends

   C. Avoiding bad publicity

   D. The impact on staff morale

8. Which of the following is not an example of ethical policies adopted by a business?

   A. Fair trading terms with businesses in low income countries

   B. Fringe benefits offered to all members of staff

   C. Sponsoring charity events in the local community

   D. The safe disposal of waste materials

9. Businesses do not always consider acting in an ethical way. Which of the following does not explain why this might be the case?

   A. Compliance costs are low

   B. Ethical objectives often conflict with profit objectives

   C. Ethics might not be important to the firm

   D. There might not be any government constraints

10. An ethical code of practice is not likely to include details concerning

   A. Corporate social responsibilities

   B. Ethical marketing practises

   C. Expectations of employees in the workplace

   D. Statutory employment rights

11. Unethical business practices do not include

   A. Deliberately using offensive tactics to market a firm's products

   B. Lending money to companies that manufacture weapons

   C. Setting higher prices to raise profit margins

   D. The production of demerit products such as alcohol, tobacco and gambling

12. What does the 'R' in SMART objectives stand for?

   A. Rational

   B. Realistic

   C. Reasonable

   D. Righteous

13. Which of the following would not be considered as a strength in a SWOT analysis for a firm?

A. A broad product portfolio

B. A high market share

C. A high staff turnover rate

D. A wide customer Sbase

14. Which of the following is least likely to be an opportunity in a SWOT analysis for a firm?

A. A merger with a rival firm

B. Entering new overseas markets

C. High levels of staff retention

D. The development of new products

15. Which of the following would not be considered as a threat in a SWOT analysis?

A. A hostile takeover bid from another company

B. Industrial action from the workforce

C. Lower entry barriers in the industry

D. Lower interest rates in the economy

16. Which of the following is not a growth option in the Ansoff Matrix?

A. Diversification

B. Market development

C. Market penetration

D. Mergers and acquisitions

17. The low-risk growth option where firms operate in a known market with familiar products is known in the Ansoff matrix as

A. Market growth

B. Market penetration

C. Market-orientation

D. Product development

18. The introduction of salads and alternative burgers at McDonald's has helped it to raise sales in existing markets. Which of Ansoff's growth strategies does this describe?

A. Diversification

B. Market development

C. Market penetration

D. Product development

19. In Ansoff's matrix, __________ ______________ is the marketing of existing products in existing markets.

- **A.** Market development
- **B.** Market growth
- **C.** Market penetration
- **D.** Market planning

20. Product extension strategies, used to prolong the demand for goods and services, are most suitable for which growth strategy?

- **A.** Diversification
- **B.** Market development
- **C.** Market penetration
- **D.** Product development

Unit 1.4 Stakeholders

Task 1: Complete the missing words

Stakeholders are __________, groups or organizations that have a direct interest in the operations and performance of an organization or are directly affected by its operations. Examples include: ______________ (owners), directors, employees, competitors, customers and suppliers.

__________ stakeholders are those that are not directly involved in a business, but have an interest in the operation of that business. Examples include customers, the ______________, suppliers, the local community and __________ groups. By contrast, __________ stakeholder groups come from within the organization, such as employees, managers and directors

Different stakeholder groups have different interests in an organization, so this is likely to cause __________ in the business. Conflict arises because a business cannot meet all the needs of all its stakeholders at the same time. For example, if customers want higher quality products, then this may come about by firms charging higher ________. However, this clearly can upset many customers.

Task 2: Stakeholder groups

Read the definitions and match them with the correct business terms from the list below.

	Stakeholder group	Examples of stakeholder group's interest
a.		To receive regular orders and for their customers to meet payment deadlines.
b.		To receive regular dividend payments, higher share prices and discounts for purchases made.
c.		Employment opportunities, financial support for events (such as sponsorship deals or charitable donations), and minimal disruptions to the environment.
d.		Good remuneration package, job security, safe working environment, and opportunities for career development.
e.		Competitive prices, safe and good quality products, after-sales care and overall value for money.
f.		Minimal risk and the ability of their customers to repay the money owed on time.

Task 3: Explain …

a. The difference between shareholders and stakeholders.

____

____

b. The difference between directors and shareholders.

____

____

c. The difference between internal and external stakeholders.

____

____

d. What Bill Gates, co-founder of Microsoft Corporation, meant by, "Your most unhappy customers are your greatest sources of learning".

____

____

e. The sources of conflict in large organizations such as Walmart or American Airlines.

____

____

f. The sorts of decisions that are made by the board of directors of a company.

____

____

____

Task 4: Multiple choice

1. Stakeholders are

- **A.** All those parties directly working in an organization and are affected by its operations
- **B.** Individuals, groups or organizations that are affected by the behaviour of businesses
- **C.** People who can influence the behaviour of businesses
- **D.** The people or organizations that own shares in the business

2. Which of the following are internal stakeholders?

- **A.** Competitors
- **B.** Creditors
- **C.** Debtors
- **D.** Stockholders

3. Which of the following stakeholder groups is classified as external stakeholders?

- **A.** Creditors
- **B.** Directors
- **C.** Employees
- **D.** Owners or shareholders

4. External stakeholders include

- **A.** Customers
- **B.** Directors
- **C.** Employees
- **D.** Shareholders

5. Which of the following stakeholder groups is least likely to be an external stakeholder?

   A. Competitors

   B. The general public

   C. The government

   D. Trade unions

6. A business might want to become involved in community projects even though there are not necessarily any direct financial gains from doing so. Which option below does *not* provide a reason for this?

   A. For staff professional development

   B. The subsequent press coverage that it may attract

   C. To boost staff morale and motivation

   D. To enhance the image of the organization

7. Which of the following is not an internal stakeholder of the Industrial and Commercial Bank of China (ICBC)?

   A. The Board of Directors

   B. The Chinese government

   C. The hourly-waged staff at ICBC

   D. The shareholders of ICBC

8. Which statement below does not apply to the shareholders of a business?

   A. They are internal stakeholders

   B. They are the owners of limited liability companies

   C. They have an interest in the operations and performance of the business

   D. They receive dividends each year based on the number of shares they hold

9. An organization of individuals who unite to further their common interest is known as a

   A. Campaigning group

   B. Labour union

   C. Pressure group

   D. Trade organization

10. Lobbying groups would not typically support

   A. Anti-smoking

   B. Deforestation

   C. The fair treatment of workers

   D. The protection of animals

11. Which of the following is least likely to be an objective of pressure groups?

A. To change government economic objectives

B. To change government policy

C. To change opinions of the general public

D. To influence business and consumer behaviour

12. How do pressure groups primarily strive to achieve their aims?

A. By getting the workforce to take industrial action

B. By lobbying the government for changes to the law

C. By organizing mass demonstrations to win public support

D. By raising as much publicity and awareness of their cause as possible

13. A socially responsible firm, might want to donate money to a charity. Shareholders of the same firm may not necessarily agree with this as it reduces their potential dividends. This is an example of

A. Compliance costs

B. Shareholder compliance

C. Stakeholder conflict

D. Unfair competition

14. Which stakeholder group is most likely to have the following interests: financial benefits, job security, working environment and continuous professional development needs?

A. Directors

B. Employees

C. Entrepreneurs

D. Managers

15. Boycotting is often used by pressure groups to

A. Create adverse publicity for a business by encouraging customers to shun (avoid or reject) the business

B. Prevent employees from being able to attend work

C. Push governments to introduce legislation desired by the pressure groups

D. Take a business to court for its socially undesirable behaviour

16. What arises because an organization cannot meet the needs of all its stakeholders at the same time?

A. Conflict

B. Lobbying

C. Miscommunication

D. Mismanagement

17. Anti-piracy advertising against the illegal downloading of music and movies would be an example of a campaign promoted by

A. Industry trade groups

B. Labour unions

C. Local communities

D. Pressure groups

18. Which statement does not apply to suppliers?

A. They are an external stakeholder group

B. They offer preferential credit terms to all their customers

C. They provide other businesses with stocks, component parts and finished goods

D. They provide support services to their clients

19. Shareholders are

A. Entitled to receive dividends each year irrespective of the profits made

B. External stakeholders of a private limited company

C. Individuals or organizations with an investment interest in a particular business

D. The owners of limited liability companies

20. Which management tool enables managers to deal with stakeholder conflict?

A. Contingency planning

B. Crisis management

C. Perception mapping

D. Stakeholder mapping

Unit 1.5 External environment

Task 1: Complete the missing words

STEEPLE analysis stands for the S_____________, T_____________, E_____________, E_____________, P_____________, L_____________ and E_____________ factors that affect businesses, all of which are beyond an individual firm's control. STEEPLE analysis gives managers an overview of the __________ business environment.

STEEPLE analysis provides a simple brainstorming framework of the external opportunities and __________ faced by a business. It promotes proactive and forward thinking, rather than static opinions based on ___________ (gut feelings). Hence, STEEPLE analysis enables managers to be more informed and prepared to deal with external influences that affect business operations.

Task 2: Explain why ...

a. A higher exchange rate can present both an economic opportunity and threat to a domestic business.

____

____

____

____

b. Sustainable inflation (which makes prices rise) does not necessarily make a person poorer.

____

____

____

____

c. The introduction of a national minimum wage may be both a threat and an opportunity for businesses.

____

____

____

____

d. Businesses that do not initiate change are still at risk due to the external business environment.

____

____

____

____

Task 3: STEEPLE analysis

a. The table below shows examples of different external factors that affect businesses. In each case, identify the correct category of STEEPLE for each of the examples below. An example has been done for you.

Example	External factor	Example	External factor
Ageing population	Social	Tariffs and quotas	
Average family size changes		Consumer protection rights	
Consumer confidence levels		Oil price changes	
E-commerce developments		Scientific development	
Employment laws		Interest rates changes	
Exchange rate fluctuations		Moral business behaviour	
Fiscal and monetary policies		Natural disasters	

b. Identify the type of external factors (i.e. the STEEPLE factors) that affect businesses from the examples below.

Type of external influence	Examples
	Consumers go 'green' and recycle in order to conserve the planet.
	Decision to spend more money on education and public health care services.
	Increasing number of older and retired people in the country.
	Interest rate hikes dampen purchase of private and commercial property.
	More businesses devote money to developing their e-commerce strategies.
	Smoking bans in restaurants, shopping malls and public parks.
	Businesses choose to adopt environmental practice and to meet their corporate social responsibilities.

Task 4: True or false?

		True/False
a.	A government is likely to raise interest rates during times of inflationary pressure.	
b.	An appreciation of the British pound (£) against the euro (€) will tend to lead to a fall in UK exports to the rest of Europe.	
c.	Chinese importers will benefit from bilateral trade if the US dollar appreciates against the Chinese yuan.	
d.	Deflation is good for the economy as prices are falling.	
e.	Falling rates of inflation will lead to lower prices in the economy.	
f.	France has a maximum working week of 35 hours. This is an example of an economic constraint on businesses in the country.	
g.	If a government attempts to reduce unemployment, it could consider cutting interest rates and/or reducing taxes.	
h.	If the exchange rate between the British pound and the Hong Kong dollar changes from £1 = \$11 to £1 = \$12, then the pound has strengthened.	
i.	Inflation will tend to damage a country's international competitiveness.	
j.	The Central Bank can boost economic growth by cutting interest rates.	

Task 5: Vocabulary quiz

All the key terms below refer to external factors that present either threats or opportunities for businesses. Identify the key term from the given definitions. *Hint*: all key terms appear in reverse alphabetical order.

	Key term	Definition
a.		As a form of protectionism, this tax is imposed on imported products (foreign goods and services). It is levied by a government to reduce the competitiveness of imports.
b.		Occurs when there has been a decline in the level of economic activity for at least two consecutive quarters (6 months), caused by lower levels of consumption and investment expenditure in the economy.
c.		Any form of government measure used to defend domestic businesses (and hence jobs) from international competition, e.g. imposing a tariff on imports.
d.		A government policy designed to control the economy by managing the money supply, mainly via changes in interest rates and exchange rates.
e.		The cost of money to consumers and firms. The higher this is, the lower the amount of borrowing tends to be, as firms delay investment projects due to the higher costs.
f.		A macroeconomic objective which measures the percentage change in the general price level of a country over the preceding 12 months.
g.		A category of tax that is charged on the sale of goods and services, e.g. VAT, GST and excise duties.
h.		An increase in the value of a country's total output of goods and services (GDP), per year.
i.		A type of tax that is paid straight from the income, wealth or profit of an individual or a business, e.g. income tax and corporate tax respectively.
j.		The series of fluctuations in the GDP of an economy over time. The phases ('recession', 'slump', 'recovery', and 'boom') are dependent on the level of employment, income and wealth in a country.

Task 6: The economic environment

a. Describe how an increase in interest rates should dampen the rate of inflation in the economy.

____

____

____

____

b. Explain why a higher exchange rate is not necessarily good for the economy.

____

____

____

____

c. Explain the positive correlation between a change in interest rates and a change in the exchange rate.

d. Outline why inflation might make a country less internationally competitive.

e. Describe how an increase in income tax rates could help to reduce inflationary pressures in a country.

f. Identify the missing labels in the diagram below:

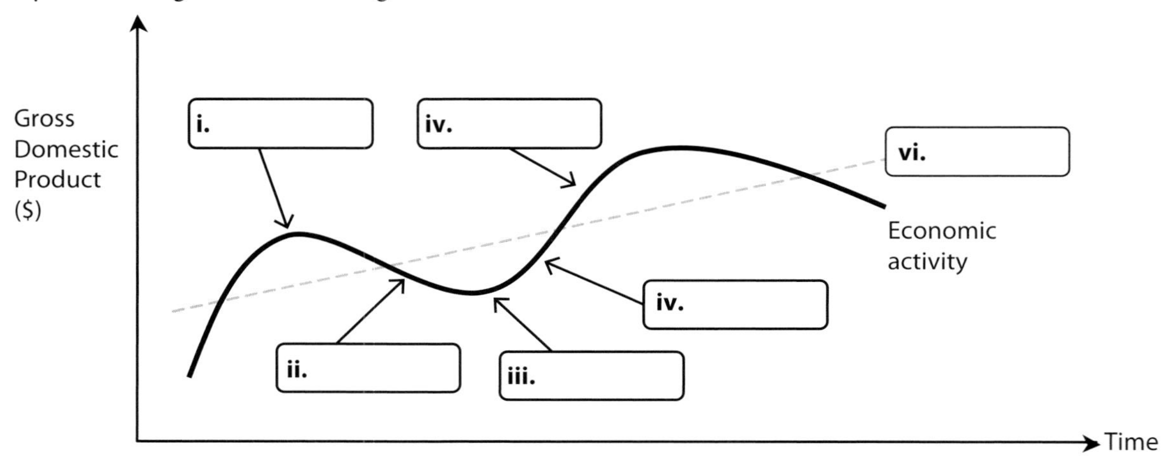

Task 7: Multiple choice

1. Which of the following is not a political factor that affects businesses?

A. Floating exchange rates

B. Import taxes

C. Legislative changes

D. The government's relationship with other nations

2. Social factors in the external business environment take account of changes in

   A. Business cycles

   B. Corporate tax rates

   C. Customs, habits and tastes

   D. Exchange rates

3. Economic variables affecting businesses exclude changes in the level of a country's

   A. Education and training

   B. Inflation

   C. International trade

   D. Unemployment

4. The study of population structures and population trends and their likely impact on business activity is known as

   A. Ageing populations

   B. Demography

   C. Social trends

   D. Social-cultural studies

5. An ethical business is unlikely to

   A. Minimise waste

   B. Pay attention to the natural environment

   C. Pay huge bonuses to its directors

   D. Treat its employees with respect

6. Which of the following strategies could be best used to deal with the problems caused by a short-term recession?

   A. Lowering prices to maintain sales revenue

   B. Moving to cheaper premises

   C. Redesign products to cater for price-sensitive customers

   D. Reducing the size of the workforce

7. Deregulation is

   A. Imposing regulations to control the activities of businesses

   B. Privatising businesses in the public sector

   C. The decline in the manufacturing sector

   D. The removal of controls in a particular industry

8. Which of the following is a direct tax?

A. Alcohol, tobacco and petrol taxes

B. Excise duties

C. Sales taxes

D. Taxes on income from interest and dividends

9. Corporate tax is an example of a(n)

A. Direct tax

B. Excise Duty

C. Import tariff

D. Indirect tax

10. Which of the following taxes is least likely to directly affect a business in the hotel and catering industry?

A. Corporate tax

B. Excise duties

C. Income tax

D. Local government taxes

11. If the exchange rate of the pound (£) changes from £1: $1.4 to £1:$1.5, then the currency has

A. Deflated

B. Floated

C. Strengthened

D. Weakened

12. Which of the following is not a valid reason for government intervention in business activity?

A. To encourage healthy competition between firms in a market

B. To protect consumers through legislation

C. To protect the environment through imposing fines on polluters

D. To supply services such as health care to compete with private sector providers

13. Fiscal policy is about

A. Changing exchange rates to influence business activity

B. Increasing the level of spending in an economy

C. Taxation and government expenditure policies

D. Using exchange rates to affect the level of spending in the economy

14. Gross domestic product measures

A. A change in prices of a representative basket of goods and services

B. The amount of a country's production each year

C. The level of unemployment in an economy during the year

D. The total value of a country's output during a year

15. Business ethics are not concerned with

A. Interest rates

B. Moral codes of practice

C. Providing a safe working environment

D. Social responsibilities

16. Inflation can be caused by

A. A fall in the level of business and consumer confidence

B. A rise in the prices of vital imported raw materials

C. An rise in a country's productive capacity

D. An increase in a country's productivity rate

17. What is the most likely consequence of higher interest rates in the economy?

A. An increase in the volume of exports

B. Higher levels of investment

C. More applications for bank loans

D. Weakened consumer spending

18. Study the table below and calculate the amount of direct tax revenue collected by the government:

	$ million
Corporation tax	52,350
Customs duties	32,550
Excise duties	42,250
Goods and Services Sales tax	63,505
Income tax	245,500

A. $245,500 million

B. $297,850 million

C. $361,355 million

D. $372,650 million

19. If a government wants to stimulate economic growth, which of the following would it be most likely to increase?

A. Exchange rates

B. Government spending

C. Income tax

D. Interest rates

20. Which of the following is not a stage in the business cycle?

A. Boom

B. Decline

C. Recession

D. Recovery

21. Which of the following is not considered to be an external constraint?

A. An oil crisis raises the production costs for most industries

B. Cash-flow problems harming international expansion plans

C. Higher than expected unemployment causing a fall in domestic sales

D. The outbreak of a war

22. Employment practices that take a more positive attitude towards women in terms of pay and promotional opportunities is an example of

A. Economic change

B. Legal change

C. Political change

D. Social change

23. Calculate the unemployment rate in a country with a population of 60 million people, of which 30 million are employed and 2 million are unemployed.

A. 3.33%

B. 5.33%

C. 6.25%

D. 6.66%

24. Using the data from Question 23 above, what is the total number of people in the workforce?

A. 28 million

B. 30 million

C. 32 million

D. 60 million

25. Which of the policies below would not be used to combat inflation?

- **A.** Appreciating the domestic currency
- **B.** Raising labour productivity
- **C.** Raising the minimum wage
- **D.** Subsidising production costs of domestic firms

26. One drawback of economic growth is

- **A.** Increased consumption expenditure
- **B.** Increased investment in the economy
- **C.** Increased rate of employment
- **D.** Increased resource depletion

27. A key difference between quotas and tariffs is that the latter method

- **A.** Is more effective in reducing the demand for goods and services
- **B.** Is seen as less aggressive as a method of protectionism
- **C.** Raises prices of imports for both customers and businesses
- **D.** Raises tax revenues for the domestic government

28. Views on the rights of women, children, animals and religions are examples of which STEEPLE factor?

- **A.** Economics
- **B.** Ethics
- **C.** Political
- **D.** Social

29. Changes in social attitudes towards climate change is an example of which STEEPLE factor?

- **A.** Environmental
- **B.** Ethics
- **C.** Legal
- **D.** Technological

30. Anti-discrimination laws are an example of which type of legislation affecting business activity?

- **A.** Competition laws
- **B.** Consumer protection legislation
- **C.** Employee protection laws
- **D.** Environmental protection legislation

Unit 1.6 Growth and evolution

Task 1: Complete the missing words

____________ growth refers to the increased size of a business by using its own resources, such as ____________ profit. It is also known as __________ growth. ____________ growth occurs when a firm expands by merging with or ____________ another firm. This method is also known as ____________ growth.

Firms looking for quick growth and expansion will tend to use ____________ growth strategies such as purchasing a majority stake in another company. This strategy is known as a ____________. By contrast, a ________ ____________ is where two or more companies share the financial risks and rewards of a business project. The firms jointly establish and own a ____________ business.

One benefit of organizational growth is ____________ of scale. These are ____________ savings due to large scale of business operations, i.e. ____________ costs of production fall as the level of ____________ increases. The main types of economies include financial, managerial, purchasing (or commercial) and marketing. The ____________ (or best) size for a business depends on its aims, the structure of its costs, and the size of the market.

Globalization refers to the growing degree of ____________ and interdependence of the world's economy. This means that decisions and actions taken in one part of the world will have direct effects on those in other parts of the world. A key contributing factor of globalization is the growth and expansion of ______________ ______________ (MNCs). There is increasing pressure for these global businesses to market their brands worldwide. ______________ progress, such as e-commerce, has also contributed to globalization by improving consumer access to a huge range of markets.

Globalization has both positive and detrimental effects on business growth and evolution, e.g. it stimulates ______________ as there are more foreign businesses and products competing in the domestic market. At the same time, the ______________ of trade restrictions has allowed domestic businesses to enter overseas markets, thereby enabling these firms to benefit from economies of scale (lower average ____________ as a firm expands its operations) and a larger ______________ base.

Task 2: Vocabulary quiz

Identify the key terms from the clues given. *Hint*: the answers are in alphabetical order.

Key term	Definition
	Often a hostile method of growth that involves buying a majority stake in another business in order to take control of the target business.
	Refers to the cost per unit of output. It is calculated by dividing total costs (TC) by the quantity of output (Q), i.e. TC ÷ Q.
	Businesses that provide a diversified range of products and operate in an array of different industries.
	Growth strategy that involves payment of an initial fee and royalty payments in return for the use of another firm's trademarks, logos and products.
	This form of external growth occurs when a business amalgamates (integrates) with another firm in the same industry.
	External growth of firms through mergers and takeovers of other businesses.
	External growth method that occurs when two or more businesses split the costs, risks, control and rewards of a business project. In doing so, they agree to set up a new legal entity.
	This is an agreement between two companies to form a single legal entity with its new or revised Board of Directors.
	An organization that operates in two or more countries, with its Head Office usually based in the home country.

Key term	Definition
	This growth strategy involves two or more firms working together on a specific business venture. They form a legally binding contract without losing their individual corporate identities.

Task 3: Economies and diseconomies of scale

a. Explain why is it relatively easier to enter the restaurant industry than to enter the pharmaceutical manufacturing industry.

b. Outline two causes of external diseconomies of scale.

c. Explain whether a firm would experience economies or diseconomies of scale given the following information: total costs of production increase from \$5000 to \$6000 following an increase in output from 200 units to 300 units, with fixed costs at \$2000.

d. Explain why 'average fixed costs' will continually fall with increased levels of output.

Task 4: True or false?

		True/False
a.	A conglomerate merger takes place between two firms that are in different lines of business.	
b.	A demerger takes place when a firm splits into smaller firms or sells a number of its subsidiaries.	
c.	A franchisee offers a franchise to a franchisor.	
d.	Conglomerates tend to be large multinational companies that operate in many countries.	
e.	Economies of scale are the reduction in costs of production achieved through increased output.	
f.	Expanding overseas is an example of diversification as a growth strategy.	
g.	Growth through horizontal mergers or acquisitions does not represent any growth in the industry.	
h.	Multinational companies are public limited companies that operate overseas.	
i.	Multinational companies can minimise their tax bills by operating in overseas countries.	
j.	Organic growth comes from increased sales revenue and profits, the latter of which is invested back in the business.	
k.	Private limited companies cannot be taken over.	

Task 5: Explain the difference between …

a. A franchisee and franchisor.

b. Acquisitions and mergers.

c. Internal and external economies of scale.

Task 6: Multiple choice

1. Internal diseconomies of scale can be caused by

   A. Being unable to purchase stocks at a discounted price

   B. Higher advertising costs to a global audience

   C. Management control being weakened with a larger workforce

   D. Traffic congestion causing delays to the delivery of inventory

2. Which of the following is not a cause of internal diseconomies of scale?

   A. Late deliveries due to congestion in busy locations

   B. Less control, direction and coordination of human resources

   C. Poor communications between different departments

   D. The lack of staff morale and motivation

3. If a firm increases its use of all factors of production but sees an increase in its average costs, this is a sign of

   A. External diseconomies of scale

   B. External economies of scale

   C. Internal diseconomies of scale

   D. Internal economies of scale

4. Internal economies of scale are those that

   A. Generate lower unit costs of production

   B. Increase due to the growth of the industry as a whole

   C. Reduce production costs in the short run

   D. Result from changes in production techniques

5. External economies of scale can arise from

   A. Bulk purchases of raw materials, parts and components at favourable prices

   B. Lower interest rates, thus reducing the cost of borrowing to larger companies

   C. Specialised back-up services available in a particular region

   D. The introduction and use of advanced technologies

6. External economies of scale are cost savings available to the whole ________ as a result of its __________.

   A. Business, location

   B. Business, size

   C. Industry, location

   D. Industry, size

7. If a firm doubles its use of factor inputs and finds that output increases by 50%, then it has experienced

   A. External diseconomies of scale

   B. External economies of scale

   C. Internal diseconomies of scale

   D. Internal economies of scale

8. If a firm increases its use of all factors of production but sees an increase in its average costs, this is a sign of

   A. External diseconomies of scale

   B. External economies of scale

   C. Internal diseconomies of scale

   D. Internal economies of scale

9. Technological economies of scale can only be feasible for a business if

   A. Banks lend money for the purchase of highly expensive technology

   B. Capital equipment is capable of producing mass units of a product in a short time

   C. There is an economic boom

   D. There is sufficient market demand for the product

10. Which one of the following is not a benefit of forming a conglomerate?

   A. Economies of scale

   B. Focused marketing

   C. Market power

   D. Spreading risks

11. In 2006, L'Oreal (the world's largest cosmetics and beauty firm) acquired The Body Shop. This is an example of

   A. A management buy-out

   B. A merger

   C. Diversification

   D. Horizontal integration

12. In 2006, Walt Disney agreed to a $7.4 billion deal to buy Pixar. This is an example of

   A. A merger

   B. A management buy-out

   C. An acquisition

   D. Horizontal integration

13. Which of the following is not a valid argument for pursuing growth as an objective?

 A. To achieve internal economies of scale
 B. To increase market share
 C. To increase the chances of business survival
 D. To minimise communication problems

14. Which one of the following is least likely to be an advantage of forming a strategic alliance?

 A. Firms enjoy some of the advantages of mergers without losing their corporate identity
 B. Profits from the strategic alliance can be shared equally
 C. Strategic alliances are founded on friendly, cooperative and mutual agreements
 D. They are not as expensive as takeovers or mergers

15. If several independent firms in the same office block share the use of a secretary and receptionist, then this is an example of a(n)

 A. Economies of scale
 B. Joint venture
 C. Organic growth
 D. Strategic alliance

16. An advantage of diversification is the

 A. Economies of scale that can be achieved
 B. Extra time and resources devoted to the new business venture
 C. Finance needed to fund the expansion plans
 D. The required expertise, such as knowledge of new markets

17. A disadvantage of diversification is the

 A. Degree of management control
 B. Entering of new markets
 C. Increased customer base
 D. Spreading of risks

18. Horizontal integration occurs when

 A. A firm acquires or merges with another firm at the same stage of production
 B. A firm acquires or merges with another firm operating in a different stage of production
 C. Ttwo or more firms that are in direct competition decide to merge
 D. Two or more firms that are not in direct competition decide to merge

19. A business grows in size due to its own finance and retained profits. This process is known as

A. A conglomerate

B. An acquisition

C. External growth

D. Organic growth

20. A franchise is the

A. Person or business selling the right for others to use their name, logos or products

B. Person who buys the right to use someone else's products, logo or brand name

C. Right to trade using another firm's products, brand name and logo

D. Uuse of methods of external growth to enlarge a multinational corporation

21. A merger between two newspaper companies is an example of

A. Conglomerate merger

B. Horizontal integration

C. Lateral amalgamation

D. Vvertical integration

22. Organic growth cannot be achieved through increased

A. Capital expenditure (investment)

B. Labour turnover

C. Prices for certain goods and services

D. Sales turnover

23. Which of the following cannot be applied to internal growth?

A. Financed through retained profits of a firm

B. Relatively cheaper method of growth

C. Relies on the production and marketing of a firm's products

D. Suitable for firms looking to grow rapidly

24. Which of the following does not explain why small firms can survive and flourish?

A. Being able to provide a personalised service

B. Choice of finance options

C. Financial aid from the government

D. Local monopoly power

25. When two different organizations contribute resources to a shared project by forming a separate business, this is known as

A. A joint venture

B. A strategic alliance

C. Collaboration

D. External growth

26. Which statement below does not apply to franchises?

A. The failure rate is low as franchisees are generally very motivated

B. The franchisee can buy or lease a franchise

C. The franchisor can expand its business without incurring huge debts

D. The franchisors have little, if any, control over the way the business operates

27. One potential disadvantage of mergers is a change in

A. Access rights to technology and human resources

B. Market power

C. Ssynergy

D. The corporate culture

28. An advantage, to the buyer, of a takeover bid includes

A. Changes to corporate cultures

B. Changes to the corporate identity

C. Possible staff redundancies

D. Potential market dominance

29. Multinational companies that market their products by expanding into overseas markets is an example of

A. Diversification

B. Market development

C. Market penetration

D. Product development

30. A firm may choose to demerge (break up) for the following reasons, except to

A. Avoid falling profits in the business

B. Enjoy economies of scale

C. Focus more specifically on a target market

D. Focus on a smaller range of products and services

31. Reasons for airlines to form a strategic alliance include all the following, except

A. The airline companies keep their separate legal identities

B. They benefit from economies of scale from combined purchasing and marketing power

C. They can cover more destinations (flight locations) by joining forces

D. They can grow through diversification

32. The process of taking over another firm's brands rather than the whole company is known as

A. Brand acquisition

B. Brand awareness

C. Brand loyalty

D. Brand recognition

33. Which of the following is a potential drawback to a multinational company expanding overseas?

A. Different business etiquette and customs

B. Opportunities for economies of scale

C. The spreading of risks by not relying on trading in any single economy

D. Wage rates in incomes countries

34. Which of the following is least likely to be a barrier to international trade?

A. Communication across geographical locations

B. Cultural differences

C. International business etiquette

D. Political and economic conflict

35. Benefits of globalization to a business include

A. Economies of scale

B. Increased market choice

C. Price transparency

D. Rivalry

Unit 1.7 Organizational planning tools *[HL Only]*

HIGHER LEVEL

Task 1: Complete the missing words

Organizational planning tools provide a systematic framework to deal with problems, concerns or issues faced by a business so that rational and sound decisions are made. For example, __________ __________ analysis is used to deal with the forces for and against change. A __________ __________ is a visual representation of the probable outcomes (in monetary terms) resulting from the various decisions that a business can pursue. Ishikawa's __________ diagram helps to establish the root causes of a business problem. __________ charts are used to minimise the resources needed in order to complete a project in the __________ time possible. Most decision making models consider the various opinions and beliefs of a firm's ____________________ (such as the shareholders, managers and employees).

Business decisions are not always made purely on facts and quantifiable reasoning. Instead, key decisions are often based on gut feelings, emotions, ______________ (or instinct) and whether managers are comfortable with their decisions, irrespective of any potential financial gains. Nevertheless, managers tend to consider both the benefits (financial and non-financial) and the costs before making any final decisions. Decision-making is also likely to be affected by various ______________ styles, e.g. it is probable that autocratic managers make decisions in a different manner from democratic or laissez-faire managers.

Task 2: True or false?

		True/False
a.	All change, no matter what size, has implications for staff.	
b.	An advantage of decision trees as a decision-making tool is that they consider qualitative aspects of a key decision.	
c.	Decision nodes are represented by squares in a decision tree diagram.	
d.	Gantt charts show the quickest time in which projects can be completed if tasks are sufficiently well-planned and carried out efficiently.	
e.	In a fishbone diagram, the problem or issue under consideration is shown on the left hand side of the diagram.	
f.	In a force field analysis, driving forces push for change whilst restraining forces act against change.	
g.	Organizational planning tools guarantee success.	
h.	Organizational planning tools help businesses to deal with their problems, issues or concerns in a systematic way.	
i.	The fishbone diagram has statistical weights placed on each cause or effect of a problem or issue.	
j.	Traditionally, a fishbone diagram shows the causes and effects of a problem or issue.	

Task 3: Multiple choice

1. Which advantage does not apply to the use of decision trees?

A. They are based on important intuitive and qualitative factors that affect decision making

B. They force managers to assess the risks made in pursuing certain decisions

C. They provide a quick and visual interpretation of the likely outcomes of decisions that need to be made

D. They set out decision-making problems in a clear and logical manner

HIGHER LEVEL

2. Which of the following is not a drawback of using decision trees?

   A. The probabilities are only estimates, so the outcomes are therefore uncertain

   B. They ignore intuitive decision-making

   C. They ignore social factors and legal constraints in the decision-making process

   D. They ignore the financial costs of investment decisions

3. Which statement does not apply to the fishbone model?

   A. It can be a useful brainstorming tool for decision-making

   B. It is a visual tool used to identify the root cause of a problem or issue

   C. It looks at the causes and effects of a particular problem or issue

   D. It places a monetary value on key decisions

4. External constraints on organizational planning include

   A. Changes in human resources

   B. Organizational culture

   C. Shocks in the external environment

   D. The availability of finance

5. At the initial stages of dealing with restraining forces, a business is most likely to

   A. Carry out a STEEPLE analysis

   B. Communicate the purpose of change

   C. Conduct a SWOT analysis

   D. Identify key barriers to change

6. Force field analysis is

   A. Not of any use to inward-looking organizations

   B. Subjective as weights can be skewed in favour of management preferences

   C. Used to examine the reasons for change

   D. Useful for examining external factors affecting change

7. To overcome resistance to change, a business is most likely to

   A. Adopt a dictatorial leadership style to implement change

   B. Communicate every stage of the change process to accelerate developments

   C. Entice staff to conform to change by promising future pay rises

   D. Hold a staff meeting to explain why the changes are necessary

8. Which of the following is unlikely to be a core feature, rather than an outcome, of effective change management?

   A. Communicating the rationale for all changes to overcome resistance to and fears of change

   B. Gaining the support for change from all staff members

   C. Providing training opportunities to cope with and adapt to the change

   D. Summarizing the net benefits of change

9. Factors that push for change in an organization are known as

   A. Competitive forces

   B. Driving forces

   C. Motivating forces

   D. Restraining forces

10. Which factor is not a cause of resistance to change?

   A. Adaptive cultures

   B. Inadequate or inaccurate information

   C. Insecurities and fears of the unknown

   D. Miscommunications

11. Which option does not suggest why the change process might fail?

   A. Empowerment of staff

   B. Inability to communicate the vision for change

   C. Inert organizational cultures

   D. Not planning for short term impacts

12. Which factor below does not present a barrier to effective change management?

   A. Individuals being unable to reach their higher level needs, such as recognition or self-actualization

   B. Managers finding it difficult to change their management style to accommodate the change

   C. The fear of change, such as job losses or reductions in remuneration

   D. Training needs to allow staff to adapt to change, although this might prove to be expensive and time consuming

13. Which statement does not apply to Gantt charts?

   A. The time scale is shown on the vertical axis of the chart

   B. They allow managers to complete a project in the quickest time available

   C. They are used to schedule tasks of a project

   D. They give project managers an instant overview of a particular project

HIGHER LEVEL

14. The rules used to construct and interpret Gantt charts do not include

A. Each bar shows the start date, duration and end date of an activity

B. Each horizontal bar shows the start and finish dates

C. Tasks that can be carried out simultaneously are combined on a bar in the chart

D. The length of each bar in the Gantt chart shows the duration of the task

15. The ultimate purpose of producing a Gantt chart is to

A. Allow managers to set out problems in a clear and logical manner

B. Identify the shortest amount of time needed to complete a particular project

C. Plan tasks in a logical sequence so that all different processes can be completed

D. Weigh up the advantages and disadvantages of a decision

Unit 2.1 Functions and evolution of human resource management

Task 1: True or false?

		True/False
a.	A zero staff turnover rate is desirable.	F
b.	Cognitive training is about training and developing the mental skills of workers in order to improve their work performance.	T
c.	Dismissal is fair if an employee is asked to leave due to incompetence or major misconduct in the workplace.	T
d.	Employees can be instantly dismissed for breaking company policy, such as turning up to work in the wrong uniform.	F
e.	Grievance can occur when there is conflict in the workplace.	T
f.	Induction training is intended for new employees to make acquaintance with the organization and key personnel.	T
g.	One benefit of training and development is lower levels of staff retention.	F
h.	The document that gives the profile of the ideal candidate for a job is called the job description.	F
i.	The main method of selection is via interview.	T

Task 2: Vocabulary quiz

Identify the key terms from the clues given. *Hint*: the answers are in alphabetical order!

a). Human resource management

Key term	Definition
	The number of people away from work as a percentage of the size of the workforce in a business, per period of time.
	a document outlining an applicant's education, employment history, skills and professional qualifications
Dismissal	The termination of an employee's employment due to incompetence (unsatisfactory performance) or a breach of contract.
HR planning	The management process of anticipating and meeting an organization's current and future staffing needs.
	The study of what is included in a job, such as the tasks, responsibilities and skills involved.
	Measures the rate of change of human resources within an organisation, per period of time.
Job description	A document detailing the required skills, qualifications and experience of the ideal candidate for a job.
	Measures the output of workers; often expressed as the output per worker.
recruitment	The process of hiring suitable workers, to ensure the best candidate is hired for a particular job or role.

b). Training, appraisal and dismissal

Key term	Definition
	Process of collecting information and evidence to assess the performance of an employee.
	Type of training that deals with improving performance in the workplace by developing desired social interactions in the workforce.
	Major act of wrong doing at work, which can lead to instant dismissal without any warning, e.g. theft, fraud, endangering others, or being under the influence of drugs or alcohol whilst at work.
	Training provided for new employees to introduce them to the premises, to meet new colleagues and to be more familiar with their new job roles.
	A form of training that happens when trainees are actually doing the job.
	A type of written description of an employee's performance at work, summarizing what s/he has done and achieved during the year.

Task 3: Explain …

a. The difference between psychometric tests and aptitude tests.

____

____

____

b. Why training and development are important to a *business*.

____

____

____

____

c. Why training and development are important for *employees*.

____

____

____

____

d. What is meant by an appraisal interview?

____

____

e. Whether an appraisal should be linked to pay.

____

____

____

f. Two advantages of internal recruitment, including the internal promotion of employees.

g. Two advantages to a business in using external recruitment.

h. Two advantages of on the job training.

i. Two disadvantages of on the job training.

j. Two benefits of low staff turnover.

Task 4: High or low?

Explain whether the following measures of personnel effectiveness should, ideally, be high or low.

a. Absenteeism

b. Labour turnover

____

____

c. Productivity

____

____

d. Wastage

____

____

e. Staff retention

____

____

Task 5: Multiple choice – Workforce planning

1. Which of the following is not a task of human resource planning?

A. Discipline and dismissal

B. Payment of wages and salaries

C. Recruitment

D. Staff retention

2. A post holder's existing job description and person specification are not used for

A. Appraisals

B. Identifying training needs

C. Job evaluation

D. Promoting employees

3. Interviews conducted by a group of interviewers all at the same time are known as

A. Face to face interviews

B. Panel interviews

C. Sequence interviews

D. Telephone interviews

4. The ability of a business to keep its employees working for the firm, rather than to seek employment elsewhere, is known as

   A. Internal recruitment

   B. Motivation

   C. Retention

   D. Selection

5. Advantages of working from home are least likely to include

   A. Ability to balance personal life and work life

   B. Autonomy in decision-making

   C. Tax allowances for using personal property for business use

   D. Time and money saved by not having to travel to and from the workplace

6. A teleworker can benefit most from

   A. Costs of electricity being shared by the employer

   B. Interactions with family members at home

   C. The absence of certain company policies such as dress code

   D. Working in isolation every day

7. Which of the following is not an effect of an ageing working population?

   A. A decline in the dependent population

   B. Changing patterns of employment and consumption

   C. Lower levels of labour productivity

   D. Reduced occupational and geographical labour mobility

8. The supply of labour for a business is least likely to be affected by

   A. An ageing population

   B. An increase in the examination standards (entry requirements) set by the industry

   C. The dynamics of the internal workforce

   D. Training and development programmes offered by the business

9. If the workforce of Baker & Geraghty Ltd is 95 people and twenty of them resign this year, then the labour turnover rate at the company is

   A. 21.05%

   B. 78.95%

   C. 20 people

   D. 75 people

10. Which of the following is likely to be a cause of high labour turnover for a business?

A. Attractive salaries and fringe benefits

B. High occupational mobility of the workforce

C. High staff morale

D. Investment in training and development

11. Which of the following is not a demographic trend in the labour market?

A. More people are taking up part-time jobs

B. More women are joining the workforce

C. More people are self-employed

D. More people are working at the office rather than from home

12. The practice that involves relocating business activities and processes abroad is known as

A. Insourcing

B. Offshoring

C. Outsourcing

D. Re-sourcing

13. Human Resources Management does not tend to deal with

E. Appraisals

F. Budgeting

G. Product design and development

A. Recruitment and selection

14. Which option below will not necessarily reduce the supply of labour within an organization?

A. Government legislation

B. Redeployment

C. Retirement

D. Rival employers

15. The transfer of a firm's operations in foreign countries back to its country of origin is called

A. Offshore outsourcing

B. Offshoring

C. Outsourcing

D. Re-shoring

16. The inability of a worker to switch from one job to another due to a lack of expertise or qualifications is known as

A. Geographical immobility

B. Labour immobility

C. Occupational immobility

D. Structural unemployment

17. Which of the following does not represent flexible working practices?

A. Homeworking

B. Part-time employment

C. Team working

D. Teleworking

18. Which statement applies to flexitime workers?

A. They are employed in a number of different jobs, carried out simultaneously

B. They are in part-time employment

C. They choose to work whenever it suits them, rather than the employer choosing

D. They must work a minimum number of hours as required by their employer

19. A business that has a relatively high staff turnover rate faces a problem of ______________.

A. Motivation

B. Recruitment

C. Retention

D. Selection

20. A ____________ specialises in a particular field or industry, has a large database of potential applicants, and takes responsibility for the advertising and interviewing of posts. In return they charge a fee for their services.

A. Careers centre

B. Headhunter

C. Job centre

D. Recruitment agency

Task 6: Multiple choice – Recruitment and selection

1. A person specification

A. Identifies the personal achievements and employment history of a candidate

B. Lists the responsibilities of the post holder

C. Looks at the essential skills and knowledge required to carry out a specific job role

D. Specifies the requirements of what the ideal person needs to do in the job

2. A person specification is unlikely to include the __________ required from the ideal candidate.
   - A. Aptitude
   - B. Experience
   - C. Responsibilities
   - D. Skills

3. Which of the following is least likely to appear in a person specification for someone working in new product design?
   - A. Innovative
   - B. Creative
   - C. Team player
   - D. Skilled in customer relations

4. A job description for a teacher is unlikely to include
   - A. A description of the role in relation to other staff in the organization
   - B. The additional duties of the teacher
   - C. The job title
   - D. The required level of teaching experience

5. Which of the following does not appear in a job description?
   - A. Job title
   - B. Main tasks and accountabilities
   - C. Responsibilities
   - D. Skills and qualifications

6. A job vacancy may arise due to
   - A. A decrease in sales revenue
   - B. Technological advances and automation
   - C. The internal promotion of a worker
   - D. Zero staff turnover

7. A workforce plan will determine what __________ exist in an organization and include a relevant job __________ and person __________ for each vacant position.
   - A. Jobs, description, statement
   - B. Jobs, outline, statement
   - C. Vacancies, description, specification
   - D. Vacancies, specification, description

8. Which of the following does not explain why businesses need to recruit workers?

   A. Existing employees leave the firm due to retirement

   B. The business is expanding due to increasing demand for its products

   C. To avoid diseconomies of scale

   D. To cover maternity and paternity leave

9. In an interview, a question such as, "What would you do if you saw a fellow worker stealing?" is an example of which type of question?

   A. Aptitude based questions

   B. Behavioural based questions

   C. Cognitive based questions

   D. Situational based questions

10. Interviews do not directly allow an employer to find out about an applicant's

    A. Ability to converse and articulate an argument

    B. Ability to perform certain tasks in the job

    C. Level of enthusiasm to do the job

    D. Work history

11. Which of the following is not a disadvantage of interviews as a form of recruitment?

    A. Detailed questions can be asked

    B. Information given might be skewed (biased or dishonest)

    C. They are time consuming

    D. They do not reveal truly whether an applicant can do the job

12. Which option is not a reason for rejecting candidates based on their application form for a job?

    A. A mismatch of skills and qualifications

    B. Insufficient work experience

    C. Low score in aptitude assessment

    D. The employer has set a limit on the number of candidates to shortlist

13. Which of the following is not a feature of flexible working patterns?

    A. A greater number of people working from home

    B. Recruitment of part-time and peripheral staff

    C. Taller hierarchical structures

    D. The use of more mobile workers

14. Which of the following is least likely to be a disadvantage for a business that experiences high labour turnover?

A. Lack of continuity or expertise

B. Lost production during recruitment, induction and training

C. The cost of recruitment and selection

D. The wages needed to pay newly recruited staff

15. The document that acts as a final safety check to confirm the information given by an applicant is correct and truthful is known as the

A. Curriculum vitae

B. Job application

C. Personal statement

D. Reference

16. Objectives of recruitment advertising do not include

A. Attracting as many applicants as possible to apply for the job

B. Dissuading unsuitable applicants

C. Informing potential candidates about job opportunities

D. Providing information about the organization to potential applicants

17. Which statement below best applies to most, if not all, recruitment advertisements?

A. They can be published internally and externally

B. They publish the salary and benefits in order to attract applicants

C. They state the requirement of a curriculum vitae from applicants

D. They show the company website for those interested in finding out more information

18. The document that outlines the work history and achievements of a job applicant is known as the

A. Application form

B. Curriculum vitae

C. Job description

D. Person specification

19. Using an existing worker to fill a vacancy of a senior position solves the problem of having to

A. Advertise the job to suitable candidates

B. Assess the suitability of a candidate to fit into the culture of the organization

C. Find a suitable employee to fill the vacancy

D. Train the new worker in the job

20. Which of the following is a drawback of using internal recruitment?

A. A potential lack of new ideas and creativity in the business

B. It reduces 'dead wood' (outdated practices) in the organization

C. The relative amount of time needed for recruitment

D. The relative cost of recruitment

21. The advertising of an internal position is most likely to be in the form of

A. A meeting

B. A newspaper announcement

C. A staff bulletin notice

D. An internet advertisement

22. In order to test or assess the ability of a candidate to do his/her job, recruiters are most likely to use

A. Aptitude testing

B. Assessment testing

C. Panel interviews

D. Psychometric testing

23. _____________ tests can be used to assess the _____________ of candidates, such as their level of motivation or their ability to handle stressful situations.

A. Aptitude, Ability

B. Aptitude, Attitude

C. Attitude, Ability

D. Psychometric, Attitude

24. Top Tutors Ltd. specialises in finding part-time and temporary work for teachers by matching the requirements of students who seek private tuition lessons. Top Tutors Ltd. is an example of a

A. Consultancy firm

B. Head hunter

C. Job Centre

D. Recruitment agency

25. Which of the following is a benefit of high staff retention?

A. New people and ideas come into the business

B. Recruitment and induction costs are reduced

C. Staffing costs are lowered

D. There is minimal continuity and stability

Task 7: Multiple choice – Training, appraisal, dismissal and redundancy

1. Which option below would not be a feature of an induction programme?

   A. Conducting an appraisal meeting

   B. Having a tour of the workplace and premises

   C. Learning about the responsibilities in the job

   D. Meeting subordinates, the line manager and new colleagues

2. Induction training is unlikely to cover

   A. Facts and figures of the organization, such as the number of employees

   B. The basics of the job for the new recruit

   C. The history and culture of the organization

   D. Upgrading of ICT skills needed for the job

3. The length and type of induction training for a worker depends on

   i. the size of the organization

   ii. the rank or position of the employee

   iii. the complexity of the job

   A. i and ii only

   B. ii and iii only

   C. i and iii

   D. All of them

4. Which of the following is least likely to be classed as a method of on the job training?

   A. Attending specialist conferences

   B. Demonstrations to show trainees how to do a particular job

   C. Job rotation within the workplace

   D. Mentoring between an experienced employee and the trainee

5. Which of the following is not a method of off the job training?

   A. Attending evening classes

   B. Attending training at a conference centre

   C. Self-study or distance learning

   D. Work shadowing

6. Off-the-job training refers to training that is

   A. Carried out for newly appointed staff

   B. Conducted at the place of work whilst the employee is not working

   C. Conducted by specialist trainers not necessarily available at the workplace

   D. Funded by the government or training colleges

7. Which of the following is not an aim of training and development?

   A. Gain a higher budget allocation for the HRM department

   B. Improve customer service and customer relations

   C. Improve the quality of people's work

   D. Match the skills of people to the needs of the organization

8. Appraisals that involve gathering information concerning the appraisee from different groups of people who work with the employee are known as

   A. 360-degree feedback

   B. Formative appraisals

   C. Self-appraisals

   D. Summative appraisals

9. One problem with appraisal methods that use rating scales is that

   A. Some traits that are scaled may not be directly relevant to job performance

   B. They are not standardised which makes comparisons very difficult

   C. They are relatively expensive to conduct compared to other appraisal methods

   D. They lack structure in design

10. Which of the following training courses would be classed as personal, rather than professional, development for a teacher of IB Business Management?

    A. Embedding Theory of Knowledge in Business Management lessons

    B. First-aid training course

    C. Raising standards in the Internal Assessment

    D. Teaching and learning strategies

11. Which term is used to describe the act of transferring a business function or activity to an organization that operates overseas?

    A. Decentralization

    B. Globalization

    C. Offshoring

    D. Outsourcing

12. Which option below cannot be used to fairly dismiss a worker?

A. Discriminatory behaviour (of the employee)

B. Grievance

C. Sleeping on the job

D. Theft

13. Gross misconduct in the workplace does not include

A. Drunk and disorderly behaviour Embezzlement

B. Embezzlement

C. Incompetence

D. Violent conduct

14. Changing an employee's terms and conditions of employment such as their working hours or their location of work so that s/he leaves the organization is considered as

A. Ad hoc dismissal

B. Constructive dismissal

C. Discrimination

D. Retrenchment

15. The difference between retrenchment and dismissal is that

A. Dismissal comes with compensation packages

B. Dismissal is voluntary

C. Retrenchment is voluntary

D. Retrenchment occurs due to no fault of the employee

16. Which of the following is not classed as dismissal?

A. Incompetence

B. Redundancy

C. Repeated lateness

D. Suspension

17. What occurs when an employer can no longer afford to hire a worker or when a job ceases to exist following the completion of a project?

A. Discrimination

B. Gross misconduct

C. Redeployment

D. Retrenchment

18. What is the term used to describe the transfer of a staff member from a department or branch that no longer requires their services to other areas of the business where a vacancy exists?

A. Involuntary redundancy

B. Redeployment

C. Retrenchment

D. Voluntary redundancy

19. What is the name given to the type of training that involves a more experienced member of staff helping someone else to progress in his/her career by gaining and developing specific skills?

A. Behavioural

B. Induction

C. Mentoring

D. Outsourcing

20. The use of external providers for certain non-core business activities is known as

A. External recruitment

B. Offshoring

C. Outsourcing

D. Portfolio workers

Unit 2.2 Organizational structure

Task 1: Complete the missing words

The ______ of control refers to the ____________ of workers that a line manager is responsible for. For example, the manager of a large department will have a _________ span of control. A manager with a _________ span of control means that he or she is responsible for relatively fewer people. There has been much debate about the ______________ (or best) size for a manager's direct span of control. There is no consensus on this as there are advantages and disadvantages to both wide and narrow spans of control.

A ___________ hierarchical structure tends to give more responsibility to workers, so can therefore lead to a higher level of motivation. ____________ occurs when a line manager passes on _________ to others to perform a role or task. The line manager retains overall _________ but the work is carried out by empowered subordinates. In contrast, a ____________ organizational structure offers greater opportunities for promotion, closer management and supervision, ____________ chains of command and a ____________ span of control.

Charles Handy's ______________ organization theory suggests that organizations face continual change and hence need to be able to adapt accordingly. The changing organization comprises of three 'leafs' of workers: ________ workers, peripheral workers and outsourced workers.

_______________ is the transfer of information from one party to another. Managers spend a significant part of their time communicating with both internal and external ___________. Effective communication enables managers and workers to have a better understanding and control of what they do. However, cultural differences have an impact on communication in an organization. For example, language proficiency, both _____________ and oral, is a highly valued communication skill in today's ever-more competitive labour market. Cultural ignorance can cause offense to others and can cause messages to be misinterpreted or misunderstood. _____________ in communication technologies also have an impact on communication in organizations, e.g. __________________ technologies have reduced the cost of domestic and international communications.

Task 2: Explain two reasons why …

a. Many firms are downsizing and delayering.

____

____

____

____

b. Effective delegation may help to motivate workers.

____

____

____

____

c. It is important for businesses to understand their informal structures.

____

____

____

____

d. A matrix structure might cause problems for a business.

____

____

____

Task 3: Crossword

Clues across

3. The official path that instructions are passed along (14)
7. Electronic form of written communication (5)
8. Such structures help to improve communication (4)
9. Personnel organized into a group (4)
10. Holding someone responsible for their actions (14)
13. The size (number) of the firm's employees (9)
16. The act of passing down authority to others (10)
19. Abbreviation for the yearly meeting held for all key stakeholders (3)
20. Person who inspires their team and staff (6)
22. A sense of duty to others in your team (14)

Clues down

1. Your direct superior in the organization (11)
2. Structure with many levels in the hierarchy (4)
4. Abbreviation for the highest ranking person in a company (3)
5. Removing layers in a hierarchy to cut costs (10)
6. Structure that caters well for part-time practices (8)
11. Teams formed naturally, through unofficial means (8)
12. The levels or ranks in an organization (9)
14. Person with authority and responsibility for staff (7)
15. Span of control that encompasses many people (4)
17. Flexible organizational structure for projects (6)
18. A particular job that needs doing (4)
21. Type of authority over those directly below you (4)

Task 4: True or false?

		True/False
a.	A drawback of tall hierarchical structures is the potential for miscommunication problems due to the large number of layers in the organization.	
b.	A driving force for delayering is to improve communication flows.	
c.	A flat organization has few layers of management.	
d.	A wide span of control requires effective delegation of authority and responsibility.	
e.	Authority cannot be delegated to subordinates.	
f.	Bureaucracy refer to official administrative rules and regulations of an organization that govern its operations.	
g.	Delegation comes with extra financial rewards, e.g. pay rises.	
h.	Line managers have a wide span of control in tall hierarchical structures.	
i.	Responsibility cannot be delegated, i.e. it always remains with the line manager.	
j.	The span of control is inversely related to the number of layers in an organization.	

Task 5: Distinguish between …

a. Accountability and responsibility.

b. The role of directors and the role of managers.

c. Hierarchical and flat structures.

Task 6: Multiple choice

1. Who is a senior manager directly accountable to?

   A. Directors

   B. Shareholders

   C. Supervisors

   D. The Chief Executive Officer (CEO)

2. The person at the top of an organizational hierarchy is known as the

   A. Chief Executive Officer

   B. Chief Operations Officer

   C. Executive Director

   D. Non-executive Director

3. Which term is used to describe the system of organizing people within a business in terms of their rank?

   A. Chain of command

   B. Decentralization

   C. Hierarchy

   D. Span of control

4. Which option is an advantage of a wide span of control?

   A. Communication is enhanced as there are more managers.

   B. It is more cost effective due to less hierarchical levels.

   C. Managers are freed to deal with other tasks.

   D. Workers become more motivated as there are promotional prospects.

5. Which of the options below is the most likely benefit of delayering to a business?

   A. Improved motivation

   B. Increased delegation to subordinates

   C. Shorter chains of command

   D. Wider spans of control

6. Which of the following features applies to organizations with flat structures?

   A. A large number of managers

   B. Good opportunities for promotion of staff

   C. Narrow spans of control

   D. Suitable when employees are multi-skilled

7. Decentralization means

   A. Informal communication between staff from various departments

   B. Orders are sent from the Board of Directors as they need to oversee corporate strategy

   C. Passing responsibility and authority away from the Board of Directors to individual departments

   D. Removing decision-making power from managers

8. As a business grows, managers need to relinquish some of their roles and responsibilities. What is this known as?

   A. Decentralization

   B. Delayering

   C. Delegation

   D. Empowerment

9. Which type of organizational structure is based on personal relationships and social networks?

   A. Centralized

   B. Hierarchical

   C. Informal

   D. Project-based

10. Groups that are not an official part of an organization but arise from people having similar interests are known as

   A. Informal groups

   B. Lobbying groups

   C. Quality circles

   D. Specialist interest groups

11. Drawbacks of informal organizational structures do not include

   A. Confidential information being exposed

   B. Misinterpretation of the correct information

   C. Reduced bureaucracy

   D. The spreading of rumours

12. Which type of flexible organizational structure is based on different departments temporarily working together to achieve an organizational objective?

   A. Decentralized structure

   B. Outsourced structure

   C. Project-based structure

   D. Shamrock structure

13. What is the term used to describe the execution of tasks that are governed by official administrative and formal rules of an organization?

A. Accountability

B. Bureaucracy

C. Centralization

D. Delegation

14. Which term is used to describe organizational decision-making power that is kept in the hands of a few people?

A. Accountability

B. Bureaucracy

C. Centralization

D. Delegation

15. Advantages of project-based organizational structures do not include

A. Decentralized decision-making

B. Flexibility

C. Improved control

D. Inter-departmental team working

16. Which of the following is a drawback of using project-based organizational structures?

A. Conflicting interest from having more than one line manager

B. Narrower spans of control

C. Reduced employee empowerment

D. Taller hierarchical structures

17. In Charles Handy's shamrock organizations, what name is given to the group consisting of full-time professional workers who are crucial to the organization's operations, survival and growth?

A. Contingent workforce

B. Core staff

C. Outsourced workers

D. Peripheral staff

18. What name is given to the group of workers consisting of part-time, temporary and portfolio workers who are employed as and when they are needed?

A. Contingent workforce

B. Core staff

C. Outsourced workers

D. Peripheral staff

19. What occurs when the size of the core workforce in the shamrock organization is reduced?

- **A.** Bureaucracy
- **B.** Decentralization
- **C.** Downsizing
- **D.** Globalization

20. The optimal organizational structure is least likely to depend on

- **A.** Management attitudes and preferences
- **B.** Organizational and corporate culture
- **C.** The chain of command in the organization
- **D.** The size of the organization

Unit 2.3 Leadership and management

Task 1: Complete the missing words

Management is the process of getting things done through other people in order to achieve the __________ and ________________ of a business. This is likely to involve planning, organizing, co-ordinating, commanding and controlling the various operations and __________ within a business.

Managers and leaders adopt different __________ to tackle organizational objectives and strategies. For example, ________________ leaders make decisions independently of others and delegate very little, if any, responsibility to their subordinates. By contrast, ________________ leaders encourage others to be involved in decision-making (by a process of consultation and consideration of the views of the workforce) before they implement any changes. ________________-________ leaders are those who have minimal direct input in the work of their staff. Instead, they allow subordinates to make their own decisions and to complete tasks in their own way. ____________________ leadership also suggests that managers and leaders must be able to change and adapt their style to different situations. Managers may adopt a ________________ approach when inducting new staff or when dealing with staff with personal difficulties.

There are various factors that influence a person's style of management and leadership. These influences include: the nature of the __________ (e.g. whether it is routine or a major undertaking that requires strategic leadership), the nature of the __________ (e.g. his/her experience, qualifications, training and personality) and the organizational ____________ (i.e. the 'way' things are done in the organization).

Task 2: Explanations

a. Outline two factors that could influence someone to adopt an autocratic leadership style.

____

____

____

____

b. What do you think management guru Warren Bennis meant when he said, "*Failing organizations are usually over-managed and under-led*".

____

____

____

____

c. Outline two core competencies that leaders must develop to be successful.

____

____

____

____

d. If a leader needs to seek the advice from others when making a key strategic decision, is this a sign of weak leadership?

____

____

____

____

Task 3: Management and Leadership Crossword

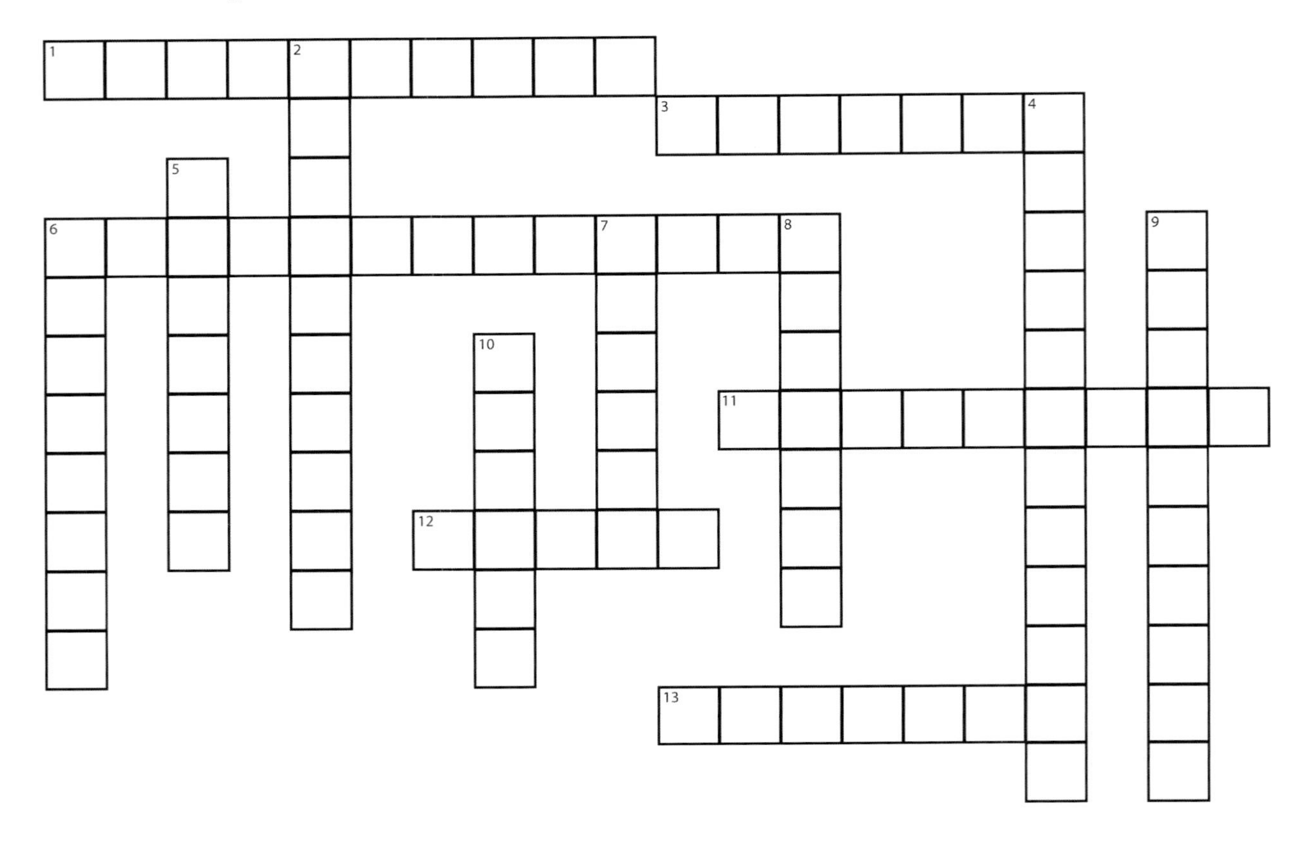

Clues across

1. An authoritarian style of management (10)
3. A key function of management (7)
6. Managers who act in a way they believe to be in the best interests of their subordinates (13)
11. Only senior managers make this type of decision (9)
12. Targets and objectives, in short, should be: specific, measurable, agreed, realistic and time constrained (5)
13. Charles Handy describes such a person to be a general practitioner, confronter of dilemmas and balancer of cultural mixes (7)

Clues down

2. One of the core functions of management as suggested by Henri Fayol (10)
4. Style of management most suited to firms with highly skilled and competent staff (12)
5. Considerations that are based on the leader's personal values and moral judgment (7)
6. All managers participate in this key function (8)
7. The highest ranking level of managers (6)
8. The customs and norms within an organization (7)
9. Management styles will affect the level of this driving force in an organization (10)
10. An official leader or manager established by the organization, rather than through natural flair or charisma (6)

Task 4: True or false?

		True/False
a.	A paternalistic management style tends to be suitable when dealing with new and inexperienced workers.	
b.	Authoritarian managers make decisions on their own without discussion or consultation with subordinates.	
c.	Autocratic leaders tend to be ineffective as they cannot motivate workers.	
d.	Corporate culture is an important factor in determining a person's management and leadership style.	
e.	Function of management include the planning, organizing, commanding, coordinating and controlling of business operations.	
f.	Laissez-faire leadership is based on managers and leaders having minimal direct input in the work of their employees.	
g.	Leaders are the people at the top of an organization.	
h.	Paternalistic leaders treat their employees as if they were family members, guiding them and acting in the best interest of their subordinates.	
i.	Since laissez-faire managers allow employees to work towards their own objectives, this tends to be the most effective management style today.	
j.	The best managers are those who are compassionate towards their staff.	
k.	The level of risks involved in decision-making is a key difference between leaders and managers.	

Task 5: Multiple choice

1. A key difference between managers and leaders is that

A. Leaders are those at the very top of an organization

B. Managers are professionally qualified

C. Managers conform to the organizational cultures

D. Managers have subordinates

2. Leadership is not directly concerned with

A. Cohesiveness in the workplace

B. Guiding people

C. Influencing people

D. Training and developing people

3. The management style that sees the leader allowing subordinates to achieve targets in their own way is known as

A. Autocratic

B. Democratic

C. Laissez-faire

D. Paternalistic

4. Which management or leadership style is most suitable during a hostile takeover?

   A. Autocratic

   B. Democratic

   C. Laissez-faire

   D. Paternalistic

5. Which statement does not apply to an autocratic style of management?

   A. It is suitable when quick decision-making is required

   B. Senior managers make all the decisions

   C. Senior managers monitor and direct workers

   D. Useful when working with highly skilled workers

6. Autocratic leaders excel when dealing with

   A. A very small number of workers

   B. An unexpected crisis

   C. Experienced workers who want to have an input

   D. Trusted employees

7. A democratic management style exists when managers

   A. Direct workers

   B. Ignore the views of subordinates

   C. Leave workers to achieve their targets in their own way

   D. Trust their employees

8. An autocratic leader does not

   A. Delegate much, if any, responsibility to subordinates

   B. Maintain overall authority in decision making

   C. Make all the decisions alone

   D. Work well during a time of emergency or crisis

9. Which leadership style encourages workers to make decisions?

   A. Democratic

   B. Paternalistic

   C. Laissez-faire

   D. Situational

10. Which of the following factors does not affect the style of management or leadership?

A. Corporate culture

B. Personality

C. Specialisation and division of labour

D. The nature of the task

11. When critical decisions need to be made, which management style is most appropriate?

A. Autocratic

B. Democratic

C. Laissez-faire

D. Paternalistic

12. Which of the following is not a feature of management advocated by Henri Fayol?

A. Authoritarian management style

B. Delegation and empowerment

C. Tall organizational structures

D. The division of labour

13. Which type of leader consults their staff and makes decisions based on such consultation?

A. Paternalistic

B. Situational

C. Laissez-faire

D. Democratic

14. Which of the following statements relates best to an autocratic manager?

A. Centralized decision-making

B. Considers the welfare of the workforce before making key decisions

C. Makes decisions that are believed to be in the best interest of the staff, even if this means being unpopular

D. Seeks the opinions of workers before making key decisions

15. According to management guru Peter Drucker, which of the following is not a key function of management?

A. Controlling people

B. Measuring performance

C. Organizing people

D. Setting clear goals

16. Which management style treat their workers as household or family members, making decisions believed to be in the best interest of their employees?

A. Authoritarian

B. Democratic

C. Paternalistic

D. Situational

17. Which management style treat their workers as household or family members, making decisions believed to be in the best interest of their employees?

A. Authoritarian

B. Democratic

C. Paternalistic

D. Situational

18. Which management style treat their workers as household or family members, making decisions believed to be in the best interest of their employees?

A. Autocratic

B. Laissez-faire

C. Paternalistic

D. Situational

19. Which management style treat their workers as household or family members, making decisions believed to be in the best interest of their employees?

A. Financial budgets

B. Organizational culture

C. The nature of the task

D. The skills and experience of the workers

20. Which management style treat their workers as household or family members, making decisions believed to be in the best interest of their employees?

A. Autocratic

B. Democratic

C. Paternalistic

D. Situational

Unit 2.4 Motivation

Task 1: Complete the missing words

Motivation refers to the ________________ (or desire) to work or to complete a particular task. This drive can come from the satisfaction of work itself (such as teaching or photography) and/or from the desire to achieve one's ____________ (such as to earn money, to gain recognition or to accomplish greatness). Methods of motivation can be classified as ______________ methods (e.g. salaries, commission and profit-related pay) and ______-______________ methods (e.g. empowerment, teamwork and job enrichment).

Poor motivation can be costly to a business because absenteeism, labour _______________, lower _______________ (output per worker), wastage and disciplinary problems are likely to increase. By contrast, high levels of motivation lead to job ________________ and improved industrial ________________.

Abraham Maslow's theory of motivation differs markedly from that of F.W. Taylor's in that _____________ considered the human side of work. He put forward the theory of a hierarchy of human needs which have to be fulfilled in order to motivate a person. At the base of the hierarchy are __________________ (basic) needs and at the top of the hierarchy are ________-_____________________ needs.

Herzberg argued that _______________ factors must be met to prevent dissatisfaction, but they alone do not motivate workers. Having a well paid job but without a sense of recognition or opportunities for _____________, Herzberg argued, does not motivate an individual. By contrast, ________________ are the factors that lead to the psychological growth of workers, and hence increase job _____________ and performance at work.

Task 2: The theorists' theories

a. Place the following examples of Herzberg's motivators and hygiene factors under the correct heading in the table below.

- Achievement
- Administration and company policies
- Advancement
- Job security
- Opportunity for promotion
- Paperwork
- Recognition
- Responsibility
- Rules and regulations
- Self-realisation
- Supervision
- Wages

Hygiene factors	Motivators

b. Arrange the following factors into Maslow's hierarchy of needs.

- Acceptance
- Accomplishment
- Achievement
- Affection
- Basic necessities
- Biological needs
- Develop fully
- Fulfil potential
- Fitting in
- Friendship
- Group identity
- Job security
- Pay
- Reputation
- Personal growth
- Predictability
- Respect
- Responsibilities
- Stability
- Status
- Steady job
- Survival

Self-actualisation	Esteem needs	Love and belonging needs	Safety needs	Physiological needs

c. Place the following considerations under the heading of the correct theorist.

- Autonomy
- Drive theory
- Effort versus reward
- Equity theory
- Mastery
- Perceived fairness
- Purpose
- Social comparison

D.H. Pink	J.S. Adams

d. Name the motivational theorist from the given clues.

Theorist	Content of theory
	Workers naturally compare their efforts or rewards to those of others in the workplace.
	Two factor theory based on hygiene factors and motivators.
	Hierarchy of needs ranging from physiological needs to self-actualisation.

Theorist	Content of theory
	People are driven by a combination of autonomy, mastery and purpose.
	Standardised output for piece rate payment based on scientific management techniques.

Task 3: True or false?

		True/False
a.	According to Herzberg, hygiene factors such as pay can cause motivation.	
b.	Contrary to what Maslow predicted, not all people want promotion or want to stretch themselves to self-actualisation.	
c.	Health insurance, company cars, paid holidays and housing allowance are examples of fringe benefits.	
d.	Herzberg argued that motivators are more important than hygiene factors to motivate a workforce.	
e.	Job enrichment means allowing employees more control over their jobs.	
f.	Overtime pay usually attracts a higher rate of pay.	
g.	Performance-related pay links payment to the level of profits of the firm.	
h.	Piece rate rewards workers who are more productive.	
i.	Pink concluded that motivation works best with financial rewards.	
j.	Taylor's scientific management considered the human aspects of the workplace.	

Task 4: Vocabulary quiz

Identify the key terms from the given definitions. All answers appear in alphabetical order.

Key term	Definition
	Sales people are often paid by this payment system which rewards employees according to the number of products they sell.
	A non-financial motivator that grants workers the authority to make various decisions and to execute their own ideas.
	These perks are received by employees in addition to their standard wage or salary, e.g. free meals and work uniforms.
	This form of motivation (and multi-skilling) involves increasing the number of tasks involved in a particular job.
	This method of motivation gives employees more responsibilities and decision-making power.
	This form of motivation involves employees working on different tasks in turn (sequence), in order to add variety to their job.
	Payment system based on rewarding individual employees who meet certain performance targets.
	This payment system pays people according to how much they actually produce or sell, thus giving workers an incentive to be more productive.

Task 5: Distinguish between …

a. Gross pay and net pay.

b. Overtime pay and bonuses.

c. Time-based and piece-rate payment systems.

d. Job enrichment and job enlargement.

e. Motivation and movement, according to Professor Frederick Herzberg.

Task 6: Explain …

a. Which of the following ought to be high (from an organization's viewpoint)?

- **i.** Absenteeism
- **ii.** Labour turnover
- **iii.** Staff retention

b. Two non-financial incentives used to motivate workers.

c. Why improved maternity and paternity rights should help to reduce the absence rate of workers with young children.

d. Why job enrichment tends to be more motivating than job enlargement or job rotation.

e. How contributions to a worker's pension (retirement) fund is an example a hygiene factor.

f. Why share options schemes may not necessarily motivate a firm's workforce.

g. How grievances and poor punctuality are both indicators of poor motivation in a business.

h. How and when each of the following leadership and management styles can motivate a workforce:

i. Autocratic

ii. Democratic

______

______

______

iii. Paternalistic.

______

______

______

i. Two advantages to a business that encourages teamwork.

______

______

______

______

Task 7: Odd one out – Herzberg

Explain which is the odd one out in each case.

a. Responsibility | Sense of achievement | Nature of the job | Work conditions

______

______

b. Wages | Supervision | Responsibility | Company policies

______

______

c. Responsibility | Company policies | Autonomy | Authority

______

______

Task 8: Multiple choice – Motivation

1. Reasons why people work do not include
   - A. To earn money to satisfy physiological needs
   - B. To feel a sense of belonging
   - C. To maintain skills and employability
   - D. To reduce absenteeism

2. A highly motivated workforce will not lead to higher levels of

   A. Customer service

   B. Labour productivity

   C. Labour turnover

   D. Product quality

3. Which scenario below is not an example of absenteeism?

   A. Chun Hoi delegates his work to an assistant as he attends all-day meetings with his team of managers

   B. Joyce does not feel well and has permission from the doctor to refrain from attending work

   C. Victor wakes up late and decides it would be better to stay at home as the boss does not like poor punctuality

   D. With consent given by his employer, Patrick attends his son's graduation ceremony

4. The theorist who suggested that workers are paid for the work that they do rather than for their mental ability was

   A. A. Maslow

   B. D.H. Pink

   C. F. Herzberg

   D. F.W. Taylor

5. Which of the following is not part of F.W. Taylor's motivation theory?

   A. Alienation of the workforce

   B. High degree of specialisation and division of labour

   C. Job satisfaction

   D. Repetitive jobs

6. Which of the following characteristics cannot be applied to Taylor's theory of scientific management?

   A. Piece rate can be used to motivate workers

   B. Workers are motivated by pay

   C. Workers are motivated by the working environment

   D. Workers specialise in order to maximise output

7. According to Taylor, what is the most effective type of payment system?

   A. Pay based on the qualifications and experience of workers

   B. Piece rate payment systems

   C. Time based payment systems

   D. Wages and salaries

8. Which statement applies to Taylor's theory of motivation?

A. Financial rewards are not enough to motivate the workforce

B. Non-financial motivators are as important as financial ones

C. Workers should be empowered to increase their level of motivation

D. Workers should specialise so that they can master their craft

9. Which statement best applies to Taylor's theory of motivation?

A. All workers are motivated by the same types of needs and wants

B. Managers regard workers as being lazy, and motivated by monetary reasons

C. Managers should closely monitor, control and supervise employees

D. Workers are motivated by job enrichment, team working and job enhancement

10. Which of the following is a maintenance factor under Herzberg's theory of motivation?

A. Advancement

B. Personal Growth

C. Responsibility

D. Salaries

11. According to F. Herzberg, which of the following is not a hygiene factor?

A. Job security

B. Policies and administration

C. Recognition

D. Status

12. According to F. Herzberg, any factor that does not directly motivate a worker, but when not present will directly demotivate someone is known as a

A. Demotivator

B. Hygiene factor

C. Motivator

D. Two-factor theory

13. According to F. Herzberg, factors that can actually motivate an employee to work harder include

A. Job security

B. Pay

C. Recognition

D. Working conditions

14. Which statement cannot be applied to A. Maslow's hierarchy of needs?

A. Lower level needs do not have to be satisfied in order for people to be motivated

B. People are not motivated by money alone

C. People's ultimate goal is self-actualisation

D. Workers can move down as well as up the hierarchy of needs

15. Several groups of people are unlikely to go through A. Maslow's hierarchy of needs in a chronological order. Which group is most likely to be the exception to this?

A. Charity volunteers

B. Freelance writers

C. Priests and other religious leaders

D. Television celebrities

16. Security needs in A. Maslow's hierarchy of needs can be met by offering employees

A. Employment contracts

B. Money (salaries and wages)

C. Piece rate payments

D. Promotional opportunities

17. According to A. Maslow, identification with and acceptance from a particular group can help to meet which level of human needs?

A. Security

B. Self esteem

C. Social

D. Survival

18. J.S. Adams' equity theory states that

A. Employees who treat their employers well will be rewarded

B. Every worker should be paid the same salary and benefits

C. Fairness exists when employers recognise efforts with rewards

D. Inequality will drive workers to perform better to secure pay rises

19. In D.H. Pink's theory, what is the term given to the desire for self-improvement to learn and create new things?

A. Autonomy

B. Drive

C. Mastery

D. Purpose

20. Making a job more challenging is an example of

A. Job enlargement

B. Job enrichment

C. Job retrenchment

D. Job rotation

21. Empowerment could be seen if a manager

A. Allocates a particular task to a team

B. Delegates decision-making authority to subordinates

C. Gives workers more jobs to complete

D. Provides more interesting jobs for workers

22. Costs of high absenteeism in the short run include all the following, except

A. The cost of hiring temporary cover staff

B. The costs of recruitment and training

C. The costs of reduced morale and teamworking

D. The loss of business due to lower productivity

23. Which statement below is not necessarily a benefit of having a highly motivated workforce?

A. Higher productivity

B. Increased rivalry among the workforce

C. Lower levels of absenteeism

D. Reduced levels of staff turnover

24. Which facility would not directly address a worker's social needs as a form of motivation?

A. Departmental offices and work areas

B. New Year party for all staff

C. Observation of anti-racial discrimination laws

D. Training and development opportunities

25. Which option is least likely to be a potential problem for James Tran Solicitors if it uses financial incentives to improve motivation at the firm?

A. It can prove to be very expensive for the partners

B. It could reduce the quality of service as solicitors now focus on output

C. It may be seen as divisive rather than promoting teamwork

D. It may encourage employees to be less productive

Task 9: Multiple choice – Motivation in practice

1. Which statement below does not necessarily apply to wages?

   A. It is a type of time based payment system

   B. It is normally paid per time period, such as per hour worked

   C. Overtime is paid at a rate higher than the wage rate for any extra hours worked

   D. Wages do not motivate workers to be extra productive

2. The payment system that rewards workers for each item that they produce or sell is known as

   A. Commission

   B. Perks

   C. Piece Rate

   D. Time Rate

3. If an employee works beyond his/her contracted hours (as shown in the contract of employment), then she/he is usually entitled to

   A. Fringe benefits

   B. Holiday pay

   C. Overtime pay

   D. Time in lieu

4. A consequence of paying workers by piece rate is that

   A. High quality work is recognised and rewarded accordingly

   B. It directly rewards people for the amount of time spent working

   C. It promotes team building

   D. Workers may ignore quality due to the emphasis on the speed of work

5. McDonald's pays its crew member staff different hourly wage rates. Which factor is not a legal justification for doing so?

   A. Different genders

   B. Different geographical locations

   C. Extent of experience

   D. Levels of responsibility

6. Which payment system is preferred for situations where quality and output cannot be easily measured?

   A. Output based

   B. Performance related pay

   C. Piece rate

   D. Time based

7. Phoebe is in a job where she is paid $15 per hour. This week, she has worked for 38 hours and has done an additional 5 hours overtime at 'time and a half' (1.5 times the contracted wage rate). Calculate her gross pay for the week.

A. $570.00

B. $607.50

C. $645.00

D. $682.50

8. Using the information in Question 7, calculate Phoebe's annual salary, excluding overtime pay.

A. $18,532

B. $29,640

C. $103,740

D. $109,915

9. The payment system whereby employees receive a share of the company's profits is known as

A. Dividend paymentsPerformance related pay

B. Performance related pay

C. Profit related pay

D. Retained profits

10. The method of motivating workers by giving them more responsibilities and more interesting tasks is known as

A. Delegation

B. Job enlargement

C. Job enrichment

D. Job rotation

11. Job enlargement is not concerned with

A. Boosting the morale of workers

B. Giving workers more complex tasks to do

C. Increasing the number of tasks performed by an employee

D. Multi-skilling the worker

12. The name given to the overall bundle of pay and perks of a job is

A. Contract of employment s

B. Payment and conditions

C. Payment systems

D. Remuneration package

13. Teamworking does not tend to allow a business to benefit from

    A. Higher labour productivity

    B. Lower absenteeism

    C. Lower labour turnover

    D. Shorter decision-making time

14. The method of motivation that encourages workers to decide on their work priorities and to come up with their own solutions to problems is known as

    A. Delegation

    B. Empowerment

    C. Job enlargement

    D. Job rotation

15. Which statement does not apply to employee share ownership schemes?

    A. Employees benefit financially if the company performs well

    B. It is used as a form of financial reward

    C. It is used as a way of retaining and motivating staff

    D. Job empowerment is granted to these employees

16. Which of the following is an advantage of piece rate?

    A. It acts as an incentive to work

    B. It encourages teamwork

    C. It is suitable for people who have autonomy in decision-making

    D. It motivates highly skilled workers

17. The non-financial motivation method that involves broadening the number of tasks that are completed by a worker is called

    A. Job description

    B. Job enlargement

    C. Job enrichment

    D. Job rotation

18. Which of the following is not a disadvantage of piece rate payment systems?

    A. There is difficulty in differentiating between the productivity of workers

    B. They are difficult to apply to many professions where measuring output is complicated

    C. They can be divisive and discourage teamwork

    D. They have a negative impact on quality as some workers take short-cuts to complete tasks

19. Which of the following is a financial method of motivation?

A. Empowerment

B. Job enlargement

C. Job enrichment

D. Medical allowances

20. Which of the following would not be classed as a fringe benefit?

A. Company car

B. Education allowance

C. Salaries

D. Work uniform (clothing)

Unit 2.5 Organization and corporate culture *[HL Only]*

Task 1: Complete the missing words

Corporate culture refers to the shared _____________, values and attitudes of the people within an organization. These norms subsequently determine the way in which the business operates on a daily basis. It also underpins corporate _______________ and influences the organization's corporate image. Senior management will seek to create a positive organizational culture in order to ______________ workers to deliver a first-rate product or service to their customers. If people are united and committed to the organization's ________________ statement, then a ___________ corporate culture will be developed.

Culture ____________ exist when there is ______________ or incompatibility between two or more cultures within an organization. This can exist when firms merge, when a business _____________ overseas (if workers are ignorant of international cultural differences) or when there is a change in ________________.

Task 2: True or false?

		True/False
a.	A culture gap tends to help strengthen corporate culture.	
b.	An understanding and awareness of organizational culture is important to managing change.	
c.	Charles Handy suggested that there is no direct link between a firm's organizational structure and its corporate culture.	
d.	Corporate culture informs employees of how things are done in an organization.	
e.	Culture frequently resembles the existing management style in an organization.	
f.	If there is a lack of trust within the organization, this provides a valid reason for a necessary change in the corporate culture.	
g.	Senior management strives to determine a corporate culture to reflect the aims and objectives of the organization.	
h.	The growth of firms through international mergers and acquisitions is a potential source of organizational conflict.	
i.	The leaders of an organization establish organizational culture through their actions and direction.	
j.	Within an organization only one culture is likely to exist.	

Task 3: Multiple choice

1. Which of the following has the largest impact on corporate culture?
   - **A.** The management and leadership styles in an organization
   - **B.** The rules and regulations set out by the prevailing government
   - **C.** The set of beliefs and values held by the people within an organization
   - **D.** The traditions and customs of a particular country

2. Cultural intelligence refers to a person's

   A. Ability to fit into a particular culture

   B. Degree of enthusiasm to blend into a culture

   C. Level of cultural awareness

   D. Willingness to comply with a particular culture

3. Although ______________ have a large part in defining and determining organizational culture, all _____________________ contribute to the culture.

   A. Directors, stakeholders

   B. Executives, employees

   C. Leaders, stockholders

   D. Shareholders, stakeholders

4. Which of the statements below does not apply to team norms?

   A. Effective interpersonal communication is critical to the functioning of the team

   B. Since team norms are well established so do not change over time

   C. Team members interact with one another based on an established culture

   D. The way in which a team makes decisions influences the degree of its success

5. When management and employees of an organization have different beliefs and values, there is said to be

   A. A culture gap

   B. An industrial dispute

   C. Conflict

   D. Corporate diversity

6. Which of the following is the least likely reason for a necessary change in corporate culture?

   A. Conflict is not being managed within the organization

   B. Profits are in decline

   C. The existing culture restricts organizational growth and evolution

   D. There is a high degree of staff absenteeism and staff turnover

7. Organizational cultural change is often met with resistance for several reasons. Which option is not one of the valid reasons?

   A. A significant event, such as a financial crisis, has occurred

   B. Employees fear change

   C. People find it difficult to change their behaviour to suit the newly desired culture

   D. Stakeholders have not been informed or consulted

8. An organization without an agreed framework for decision-making is likely to face the potential of

A. Industrial action

B. Misunderstandings and conflict

C. Prompt decision-making

D. Redundancies and retrenchment

9. An organization with one dominant decision-making individual or group has what type of culture?

A. Person culture

B. Power culture

C. Role culture

D. Task culture

10. Which type of culture is resistant to organizational change because people hold negative views about change?

A. Adaptive cultures

B. Command and rule cultures

C. Inert cultures

D. Process cultures

11. In Hofstede's model of organizational culture, what is the term used to measure the extent to which people feel they should care for themselves or be cared for by others in society?

A. Individualism versus collectivism

B. Masculinity versus femininity

C. Power distance

D. Uncertainty avoidance

12. According to Deal and Kennedy, which model of organizational culture best describes fast-paced, high-risk and high-stress organizations such as financial markets, the police force and professional sports clubs?

A. Bet-the-company culture

B. Process culture

C. Tough guy macho culture

D. Work-hard, play-hard culture

13. Which of the following is least likely to be a cause of cultural clashes?

A. A change in the senior leadership team

B. A common language of communication within the organization

C. A hostile takeover from a rival company

D. Inorganic growth and evolution of the organization

HIGHER LEVEL

14. Which of the reasons below best describes how organizational culture influences individuals in an organization?

A. Centralized decision-making, whereby managers keep hold of authority and control

B. Individual leaders can have a huge influence on organizational culture

C. Strong and established culture shaped by an individual, such as a school principal

D. The various mix of ethnicity, languages and gender within an organization

15. Which of the following is not a consequence of cultural clashes?

A. Demoralised and motivated workers

B. High costs of training workers

C. Misunderstandings and miscommunications in the workplace

D. Past rivalries between workers

Unit 2.6 Industrial and employee relations *[HL Only]*

Task 1: Explain one reason why …

a. Corporate culture affects the degree of employer and employee relations at work.

b. Conflict might exist in the workplace.

c. Workers might join a trade union (labour union).

d. Reducing or minimising conflict in the workplace is in the best interest of an organization.

e. There has been a decline in union membership in many parts of the world.

f. Avoidance is a source of conflict resolution.

HIGHER LEVEL

Task 2: Explain the difference between …

a. Conciliation and arbitration.

b. Consultation and negotiations.

c. Closures and lock-outs.

d. Industrial action and strike action.

e. Work to rule and go slows.

Task 3: Multiple choice

1. Conflict is unlikely to be caused by which of the factors below?

   A. Compromises between different stakeholders

   B. Disagreements between different stakeholder groups

   C. Incompatibilities between various stakeholders

   D. Internal politics in the workplace

2. Unmanaged conflict can become a problem for businesses. Which of the following is unlikely to result from conflict in the workplace?

   A. Higher absenteeism

   B. Higher capacity utilization

   C. Industrial action

   D. Lower staff morale

3. Which of the following is not considered to be a form of industrial action?

   A. Go slow

   B. Renegotiations

   C. Strike action

   D. Work-to-rule

4. Trade unions do not have a direct role in

   A. Collective bargaining

   B. Counselling

   C. Mediation

   D. Negotiations

5. The power of a labour union is not necessarily strengthened by which factor?

   A. Government legislation

   B. Public understanding and support

   C. The number of members

   D. The quality of the leadership of the union

6. Employees who follow all the policies and procedures with the objective of disrupting production are engaged in which form of industrial action?

   A. Go-slow

   B. Overtime ban

   C. Voluntary strike action

   D. Work-to-rule

HIGHER LEVEL

7. The negotiations and relationship between trade union members and their employer is known as

   A. Arbitration

   B. Collective bargaining

   C. Conciliation

   D. Industrial relations

8. The process by which pay and conditions of work are settled by negotiations between employers and employees, or by their respective representatives, is known as

   A. Arbitration

   B. Collective bargaining

   C. Conciliation

   D. Renegotiation

9. A directive from a trade union instructing its members to disengage in working beyond their contracted hours of work is known as

   A. Go-slow

   B. Overtime ban

   C. Strike action

   D. Work-to-rule

10. Conciliation does not consider

   A. Cooperation

   B. Litigation

   C. Negotiations

   D. Win-win situations

11. Arbitration is the process of

   A. Improving working conditions to benefit both employers and employees

   B. Resolving conflict by hiring a mediator to advise on the outcome of a dispute

   C. Settling disputes by using an agreed third party whose decision is legally binding

   D. Using an external arbitrator to negotiate a win-win outcome for those in conflict

12. Employers' associations

   A. Deal with public relations issues in order to gain positive media coverage

   B. Employ highly skilled managers to intimidate or pressure employees to cease any form of industrial action

   C. Represent the views and interests of businesses within a specific industry

   D. Represent the views of the media regarding an employer's treatment of its workers

13. Which of the following is not considered to be a reason for resistance to change in the workplace?

A. Industrial democracy

B. Low tolerance

C. Misinformation

D. Self-interest

14. Individuals or organizations that represent the management team in the collective bargaining process are called

A. Employer representatives

B. Industrial democracy

C. Single-union agreement

D. Trade unions

15. A no-strike agreement is an example of

A. Conflict resolution

B. Industrial action

C. Industrial democracy

D. Work-to-rule

Unit 3.1 Sources of finance

Task 1: Classification of assets and liabilities

Classify the following into either assets or liabilities and whether they represent an expense or a source of income for a large book publisher. Use ticks (✓) to indicate your answers.

Category	Asset	Liability	Expense	Revenue
Bank interest receivable	✓			✓
Bank loan interest		✓	✓	
Bank loans	✓		✓	
Bank overdrafts	✓		✓	
Debentures				
Insurance premiums				
Motor vehicles	✓		✓	
Rent accruals				
Retained profits	✓			✓

Task 2: Vocabulary quiz

Identify the key terms from the clues given. *Hint*: the answers are in reverse alphabetical order!

Key term	Definition
Venture capitalist	High-risk capital invested by specialist finance firms, usually at the start of a business idea, usually in the form of loans and/or shares in the business.
Working capital	The day-to-day spending required for the running of a business, e.g. rent, raw materials, wages and utility bills.
	The most common type of shares issued by a limited company, which gives owners voting rights and dividends based on the company's profits.
Mortgage	A long term source of finance which requires the borrower to provide property and land as collateral (security guarantee) to the lender in case the borrower defaults on the loan.
Internal	Refers to the generation of finance from within an organization's own resources and funds, e.g. retained profit and the sale of assets.
IPO	Refers to the original sales of a company's shares on a listed stock exchange, by offering its shares to the general public for the first time.
	This source of credit finance allows firms the chance to use assets without having to pay for them in one lump sum. Once the final repayment (instalment) has been made, the asset legally belongs to the business.
loan	A long term source of external finance which gives holders a fixed rate of return (interest) but without any ownership or voting rights.
Capital expenditure	The spending on items considered as fixed assets, such as: land, buildings, machinery and motor vehicles.
Angel investor	These are wealthy entrepreneurs who risk their own money by investing in small to medium sized businesses that have high growth potential.

Task 3: Outline the differences between …

a. Capital expenditure and revenue expenditure.

Capital → long term fixed assets
Revenue → day-to-day spending to run the business

b. Short-term and long-term finance.

Short: up to a year
long: 5+ years

c. An overdraft and a bank loan.

An overdraft is when you're permitted to spend more $ than in the bank acc.
A loan is seperate from the acc and is a set amount of $ that is repaid with interest.

d. A loan and a mortgage.

A loan can be long or short term
A mortgage is long-term and an asset must be used as collateral.

e. Ordinary shares and debentures.

Debentures (repaid) → $ provided by other businesses
don't gain voting rights (fixed rate of return)
Shares → Investors gain ownership of company

f. Debt finance and equity finance.

Equity → selling of shares eg. angel investors, ordinary shares
→ lose control / money not paid back usually
debt → $ is given to business that must be repaid with interest

g. Owners' capital and loan capital.

Owners' capital → personal funds from owner
loan capital → external source + repaid

Task 4: True or false?

		True/False
a.	A share issue by an existing company is considered to be an internal source of finance.;	F
b.	Capital expenditure is used to pay for the working capital of an organization.	F
c.	Collateral acts as security to the lender in case debtors default on their loans.	T
d.	Directors own the money of incorporated companies and use these on behalf of their shareholders.	
e.	Government grants and subsidies are sources of external finance.	
f.	It is best if a business limits external financing from a variety of sources simply because this raises its financial risks.	
g.	Overdrafts are easier to obtain than most other forms of external finance.	
h.	Permanent capital is equal to the value of shareholders' funds, i.e. share capital.	
i.	Personal finance is the cheapest source of finance.	
j.	Relying on loan capital means the business is likely to suffer during times of rising interest rates.	
k.	Venture capitalists tend to invest their money in medium to large sized businesses since they have the best investment track record.	

Task 5: Multiple choice

1. Which of the following is the most suitable reason for using personal finance?

   A. Insufficient external sources of finance

   B. Insufficient internal sources of finance

   C. No interest obligations

   D. To please the owners (shareholders) of a company

2. Which of the following is not a feasible source of finance for an ordinary partnership?

   A. Debt factoring

   B. Initial public offering

   C. Sale and leaseback

   D. Secured bank loans

3. Which of the following is not an advantage of internal finance?

   A. Administrative procedures can be avoided

   B. Greater choice of finance

   C. Greater flexibility in the use of finance

   D. Tax concessions using internal profits

4. Which of the following is the most feasible advantage of using internal funds to purchase a new office building?

   A. Increased value of fixed assets

   B. Limited impact on the firm's working capital

   C. Lower level of gearing

   D. The dilution of ownership

5. Businesses might choose to use external sources of finance because

   A. Potential cash flow problems are avoided

   B. There are no interest charges

   C. There is an expected rise in interest rates

   D. There is insufficient retained profit

6. Which of the following is not a source of external financing for a public limited company?

   A. Debentures

   B. Overdraft

   C. Retained profits

   D. Share capital

7. Advantages of funding growth through a share issue include all those listed below except

   A. An extra source of finance

   B. Control of the company becomes diluted

   C. It acts as a form of motivation for employees who own shares in the company

   D. There is less financial risk amongst shareholders

8. Which of the following is a drawback to a business that issues debentures?

   A. Investors do not have any voting rights

   B. Ownership is diluted

   C. The value of liabilities increases

   D. There is dilution of control

9. Debenture holders

   A. Are paid a return from the profits of the company

   B. Are represented as current liabilities on the company's balance sheet

   C. Own a part of the company in which they hold debentures

   D. Receive payments from companies before any shareholders

10. Debentures can best be described as a form of

A. Long term loan with a fixed interest rate

B. Long term security giving the holder part ownership of the business

C. Medium term loan with fixed interest rates

D. Short term loan with variable interest rates

11. Which of the following is not a clear difference between debenture holders and shareholders of a company?

A. Impact on the company's working capital

B. Interest and dividends as a form of financial return

C. Ownership of the company

D. Voting rights in the company

12. Which of the following is the least likely source of funds for a non-profit organization?

A. Brand recognition

B. Charitable donations

C. Fund-raising events

D. Sponsorship deals

13. Which of the following best describes hire purchase?

A. Differs from leasing in that ownership occurs with the last instalment

B. Hiring out equipment as a source of finance

C. Repaying loans by making fixed regular payments

D. The hiring of equipment for a period of time

14. The contract used to raise finance by selling the freehold of an asset and then renting it back immediately on a long-term basis is known as

A. Fixed assets

B. Sale and leaseback

C. Trade creditors

D. Working capital

15. Which statement does not apply to the use of sale and leaseback?

A. The finance released through the sale improves the firm's liquidity position

B. The firm can carry on trading as if nothing has happened

C. The firm can continue to use the asset it has sold and leased back

D. The value of fixed assets remains unchanged as the firm keeps use of the asset

16. The debt factoring service that allows the client to be protected against bad debts is known as

A. Collateral

B. Discount factor

C. Non-recourse factoring

D. Overdraft

17. Hai Ling Photography Corp. has a cash flow deficit of $85 000. If it has debtors to the value of $100 000 on its balance sheet, what is the maximum charge that a factoring service could impose to make this source of finance feasible?

A. 5%

B. 10%

C. 15%

D. 20%

18. Which source of finance below would best be described as loan capital?

A. Debentures

B. Debt factoring

C. Equity finance

D. Ordinary share capital

19. There must be sufficient finance to pay for the daily running of the business. This money is known as

A. Accumulated retained profit

B. Buffer stocks

C. Working capital

D. Work-in-progress

20. Which of the following is a disadvantage of leasing capital equipment?

A. Capital equipment needs replacing if technology is changing rapidly

B. It is cheaper in the long run to buy capital equipment

C. The firm might not have sufficient funds to purchase the equipment

D. The management of cash flow is easier with regular repayments

Unit 3.2 Costs and revenues

Task 1: Vocabulary quiz

Identify the key terms from the clues given. *Hint*: the answers are in alphabetical order.

Key term	Definition
	The sum of money incurred by a business in the production process.
	These are the costs that are clearly attributed to the production of a particular good or service.
	These production costs, such as loan repayments and salaries, do not change with the level of output.
	Also known as overhead costs, these costs cannot be clearly or easily attributed to the output of a particular product or department.
	Also known as the average revenue, this is the amount of money a product is sold for, i.e. the amount paid by the customer.
	The funds (money) received from the sale of a firm's output.
	The various sources of income generated from different business activities, e.g. sponsorship deals, merchandise income, membership fees and royalties.
	Type of costs that has an element of both fixed costs and variable costs, e.g. power and electricity or salaried staff who also earn commission.
	This refers to the aggregate amount of money spent on production for any given level of output.
	The sum of all revenue streams for a business. It is calculate by multiplying the selling price of a product with the quantity sold.
	Also known as average costs, this concept is calculated by dividing the total costs of production by the level of output.
	Costs incurred directly from the production and sale of a particular product, e.g. raw materials and packaging costs.

Task 2: Calculations

a. Wallets-R-Us Ltd. has fixed overheads of $500 and sells 250 units of output per month. Each item sells for $35, with $15 of direct costs.

i. Calculate the total costs per month for Wallets-R-Us Ltd.

ii. Calculate the company's monthly profit.

iii. Calculate the change in the average cost of production at 150 units and 250 units of output. Comment on why the unit cost has dropped.

b. Chen's Candies has monthly fixed costs of $3000 and unit variable costs of $2. Its current level of demand is 3000 units each month. The average unit price is $6.

i. Calculate the firm's current average costs each month.

ii. Calculate the margin of safety for Chen's Candies.

c. The following data refers to the costs and revenues of Sangu Toys Ltd. when operating at 2000 units of output per month:

Item	Costs and revenues ($)
Price	$15
Raw materials per unit	$5
Overheads	$500
Rent	$2000
Salaries	$3000

i. Calculate the total cost of producing 2000 units of toys.

ii. Calculate the profit made by Sangu Toys Ltd. if it manages to sell all of its output.

d. Rhapsody Sounds produces miniature speakers with the following monthly cost structures:

Total output (speakers)	Total costs ($)
100	$5 000
200	$8 000
300	$11 000

i. Assuming constant unit costs, what is the value of the monthly fixed costs for Rhapsody Sounds?

ii. What is the change in average costs of production if Rhapsody Sounds changes from producing 100 units per month to 300 units per month?

____

____

iii. If Rhapsody Sounds manages to produce and sell 200 units per month and wishes to make a 150% profit margin, what price should each unit be sold for?

____

____

Task 3: True or false?

		True/False
a.	Advertising costs tend to be considered as a variable cost of production.	
b.	Average costs of production will always fall when the level of output increases.	
c.	Average revenue is mathematically the same as the price per unit.	
d.	Donations are financial gifts from individuals or other organizations to an organization.	
e.	Economies of scale are likely to reduce the overall costs of production for a firm.	
f.	Fixed costs are those that do not change.	
g.	Rent and advertising costs are considered as fixed costs for most businesses.	
h.	Semi-variable costs are those that have an element of both fixed costs and variable costs.	
i.	Variable costs change with the level of output.	
j.	Wages, salaries, insurance premiums and the cost of purchasing stock are examples of running costs.	

Task 4: Explain …

a. The difference between fixed costs and variable costs.

____

____

____

b. Why average fixed costs (AFC) will continually fall with increased levels of output.

____

____

____

c. Two alternative revenue streams for a business.

____

____

____

____

Task 5: What type of cost?

Identify the following costs as either fixed, variable or semi-variable costs for a restaurant with a take-away service by placing a tick (✓) for each example of costs in the table below.

Type of cost	Fixed	Variable	Semi-variable
Advertising/promotional materials			
Equipment and tools			
Food supplies			
Fuel for meal deliveries			
Furniture (e.g. tables and chairs)			
Market research			
Telephone bills			
Packaging materials			
Rent on premises and buildings			
Staff salaries			
Staff wages			
Utility bills (e.g. gas and electricity)			
Vehicles (e.g. delivery cars)			

Task 6: Cost and revenue formulae

Identify the category of cost or revenue from the given formulae. *Hint*: answers appear in alphabetical order.

Type of Cost / Revenue	Formula
	Total costs ÷ Quantity produced
	Total fixed costs ÷ Quantity produced
	Total revenue ÷ Quantity sold
	Total fixed costs + Total variable costs
	Unit price × Quantity sold

Task 7: Multiple choice

1. Costs that are totally independent of the output level are known as

A. Direct costs

B. Fixed costs

C. Semi-variable costs

D. Variable costs

2. Which of the following items is not classified as an expense?

   A. Cost of postage
   B. Electricity bills
   C. Raw material costs
   D. Stationery costs

3. Which of the following is not a fixed cost for a cinema?

   A. Air conditioning bills
   B. Bank loan repayments
   C. Rent to the land owner
   D. Staff wages

4. Identify the start-up cost from the list below.

   A. Communications equipment
   B. Packaging materials
   C. Raw materials purchase
   D. Utility bills

5. Identify the running cost (on-going costs) from the options below.

   A. Cost of licenses and permits
   B. Deposit for purchasing a building
   C. Interest on bank loans
   D. Purchase of furniture, fixtures and fittings

6. Costs that are incurred as a result of production are known as

   A. Indirect costs
   B. Overheads
   C. Semi-variable costs
   D. Variable costs

7. Examples of variable costs for a motor vehicle manufacturer do not include

   A. Buildings insurance costs
   B. Costs of component parts
   C. Costs of purchasing raw materials
   D. Piece rate payment to workers

8. As the production level of a firm increases, which cost will fall continuously?

A. Average fixed costs

B. Average total costs

C. Average variable costs

D. Costs per unit

9. Overheads are best described as

A. Costs from non-operating activities

B. Costs that are fixed in the short run

C. Costs that must be paid to generate output

D. Costs that vary with the level of output

10. If you were given the 'Average' (e.g. average cost), which other variable would be required to determine the 'Total' (e.g. total costs)?

A. Currency

B. Price

C. Quantity

D. Unit of measurement

11. If a product has a selling price of $10, average variable costs of $4, and a sales volume of 1200 per period of time, then the total revenue for this time period is

A. $10

B. $4,800

C. $7,200

D. $12,000

12. If a firm has total costs of $2000 and fixed costs of $1100 for an output level of 600 units, then the average variable costs must be

A. $0.67

B. $1.50

C. $1.83

D. $3.33

13. Calculate the fixed costs of production from the table below.

Output	Variable cost ($)	Total costs ($)
10	1,500	3,845
15	2,250	4,595

A. $750

B. $1,500

C. $1,595

D. $2,345

14. What is the change in average costs of production if total costs increase from $5000 to $6000 following an increase in output from 200 units to 300 units, with fixed costs at $2000?

A. $5

B. $10

C. $20

D. $25

15. Which cost curve is shown in the diagram?

A. Average costs

B. Average fixed costs

C. Average total costs

D. Average variable costs

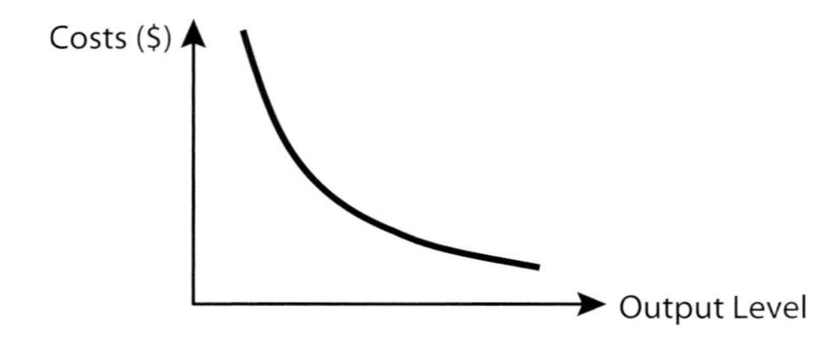

Unit 3.3 Break-even analysis

Task 1: Complete the missing words

Break-even occurs when a firm's ___________ revenue equals its ___________ costs. The firm will make a ________ if it operates below its break-even level of output. By contrast, if it is able to generate more ___________ than costs incurred in production, then it will make a __________. Profit is the positive difference between sales revenues and the ___________ of production, i.e. total revenues ___________ total costs.

To calculate break-even, it is common to use the _________________ method by dividing the ___________ costs by the difference between the product's selling price and its ____________ costs of production. For example, if a manufacturer has fixed costs of $5000 per month, with an average variable cost of $15 and a selling price of $235, then its break-even level of output would be __________ units per month. Contribution analysis can help a business to identify products or projects that are relatively profitable and ones that might need more attention.

Task 2: True or false?

		True/False
a.	A weakness of break-even analysis is that firms may have to, in reality, lower their prices to sell more units of output.	
b.	As the price of a product increases, the break-even level of output will fall.	
c.	Cutting price will mean more sales and therefore a firm can reach its break-even point quicker.	
d.	If selling price is $10, unit variable costs are $4 and fixed costs are $9,000 then the break-even level of output is 1,400 units.	
e.	Profit can be calculated using the formula: Total contribution – Total Fixed Costs.	
f.	The margin of safety can be negative.	
g.	The usefulness of break-even analysis depends on the manager's accuracy in predicting costs, revenues and production levels.	
h.	Unit contribution is calculated using the formula: Price – Unit variable costs.	
i.	When total costs rise, the margin of safety will fall.	
j.	When variable costs rise, the break-even level of output will fall.	

Task 3: Calculating break-even

Smash Racquets Co. makes a profit of $20,000 on sales revenue of $60,000. Its fixed costs are $10,000 and sales volume is 1000 units per month. Calculate the following for Smash Racquets:

a. Selling price.

____

____

b. Variable cost per unit.

____

____

c. Break-even level of output.

____

____

d. The margin of safety if Smash Racquets Co. expects to sell 500 units per month

Questions 3e and 3f refer to the following information.

Fit-it Tyres Ltd. has fixed costs of $100 000. Its average selling price is $40 with unit variable costs of $15. Use this information to calculate its:

e. Unit contribution.

f. Break-even level of output.

g. Complete the missing labels in the break-even chart below.

i.

ii.

iii.

iv.

v.

vi.

vii.

h. Explain why it is difficult to construct a break-even analysis for a multi-product firm.

i. Outline two possible causes of a fall in a firm's margin of safety.

Task 4: Multiple choice

1. Which of the following is not a direct cost of production for a car manufacturer?

   A. Depreciation of machinery

   B. Factory rental costs

   C. Production workers' wages

   D. Raw materials

2. Which of the following is a direct cost to a computer retailer?

   A. Advertising costs

   B. After-sales care

   C. Depreciation of vehicles

   D. Rental costs

3. Contribution per unit is calculated by __________ price minus the __________ variable costs.

   A. Average, Total

   B. Selling, Average

   C. Selling, Total

   D. Total, Average

4. Contribution per unit is calculated by using the formula

   A. Price minus average fixed costs

   B. Price minus average variable costs

   C. Total revenue minus total costs

   D. Total revenue equals total costs

5. Total contribution is the difference between

   A. Total revenue and total variable costs

   B. Total revenue and total costs

   C. Price and total costs

   D. Price and variable costs

6. Which of the following is a strength of break-even analysis?

   A. It assumes that all the output is sold

   B. It accounts for variances in actual sales and planned output

   C. It assumes that all output is sold at one price

   D. It accounts for both fixed and variable costs

7. A premium hotel can raise its revenues in a number of ways, except for:

   A. Reducing fixed costs

   B. Reducing its prices

   C. Reducing labour costs

   D. Raising prices during peak periods

8. What can be worked out from calculating the price of a product and its variable costs?

   A. Total contribution

   B. Unit contribution

   C. Break-even point

   D. Profit per unit

9. A firm has sales revenue of $5 million from sales volume of 4000 units. Its average costs are $600. Fixed costs are $1 million. What is the total contribution for the firm?

   A. $1.6 million

   B. $2.4 million

   C. $2.6 million

   D. $3.6 million

10. Which of the following costs will continually decline for a taxi driver as the mileage covered increases?

   A. Total variable costs

   B. Total fixed costs

   C. Average variable costs

   D. Average fixed costs

11. Any output sold ___________ the break-even point will generate a ___________ for the business.

   A. Near, Loss

   B. Above, Profit

   C. Above, Loss

   D. Below, Profit

12. If a business raises its price, which of the following is most likely to occur?

   A. Break-even output will fall

   B. Break-even output will rise

   C. Profits will fall

   D. Profits will increase

13. Which of the following statements applies to the margin of safety?

A. It can be increased if a firm becomes more liquid

B. The firm does not make a profit or a loss

C. The firm operates at a level higher than its break-even

D. The firm produces at the break-even level of output

Questions 14–17 refer to the following information.

Parc Oasis Ltd. has fixed costs of $15,000 per month, with unit variable costs of $200 and a selling price of $500 per unit.

14. What is the total cost of production to Parc Oasis Ltd. if it produces 100 units of output each month?

A. $15,200

B. $15,700

C. $35,000

D. $65,000

15. What is the average cost of producing 200 units per month?

A. $275

B. $500

C. $40,000

D. $55,000

16. What is Parc Oasis Ltd.'s break-even level of output per month?

A. 21

B. 30

C. 50

D. 75

17. If Parc Oasis Ltd. wanted to earn a profit of $50 000 on the sale of 100 units per month, what selling price should be set?

A. $500

B. $575

C. $700

D. $850

Questions 18–21 refer to the following information.

Jade Villa offers holiday accommodation at a beach resort. It has fixed costs of $22 500 per time period. The variable cost per letting averages at $250.

18. If the average villa is let out (hired) for $1000, how many villas must the firm hire out to break-even?

A. 23

B. 25

C. 30

D. 32

19. What is the value of Jade Villa's total revenue at the break-even point?

A. $22,500

B. $25,000

C. $28,500

D. $30,000

20. If Jade Villa hires out 50 villas per time period, what is the average cost per letting?

A. $250

B. $450

C. $700

D. $1,000

21. If Jade Villa planned to earn a contribution of $1000 per letting, what price should it charge, on average?

A. $1,000

B. $1,250

C. $2,000

D. $2,275

22. Which of the following is not an assumption of break-even analysis?

A. Variable costs per unit are constant

B. Economies of scale can only occur as the firm expands output

C. Productivity levels are held constant

D. Forecasts are only as good as the data used to make the predictions

23. A key limitation of break-even analysis is that

A. Average fixed costs are very difficult to calculate in reality

B. Calculating the desired contribution at different sales levels is cumbersome

C. It cannot allow for changes in fixed costs of production

D. It is a static model that does not cater well for the dynamic nature of business

24. Which of the following is not a criticism of using break-even analysis?

A. In reality, costs are unlikely to be linear

B. Multi-product firms cannot make use of break-even analysis

C. Prices are unlikely to be constant across all levels of sales

D. Unit costs are unlikely to remain constant across all levels of output

25. The concept of break-even analysis can help in the following business decisions, except for

A. Make or buy decisions

B. The payback period (investment appraisal)

C. Qualitative decision-making

D. Special order decisions

Unit 3.4 Final accounts

Task 1: Complete the missing words

All businesses need to be accountable to their owners. One way to do this is to produce final accounts on an _______ basis. The _________ _____ shows a snapshot of a firm's assets and liabilities at a particular point in time (usually at the end of the trading year). _______ are the property of a business, i.e. the resources that it owns. _______ are the monies owed by the firm to other people or organizations.

The _______ and _____ account is a record of the firm's trading activities over a period of time (usually ___ months). It is split into three parts. The _______ account shows the value of a firm's gross profits, i.e. the difference between sales revenues and the cost of ______ (or the _______ of goods sold). _________ are the overheads of a business that account for the difference between a firm's ______ profit and its net profit. The remaining part of the account shows the amount of ___________ distributed to shareholders and the _______ payable to the government.

When reporting fixed assets, some businesses include ____________ assets. These are non-physical assets that have a monetary value, such as __________, _____________, brand value and investments in other companies.

When compiling the final accounts, businesses must abide by the ____________ and ethics of accounting practice, as established by a regulatory body. Examples include: ____________ (honesty), ____________ (free from bias), ethics, confidentiality, and professional conduct

Higher Level Only:

_________ refers to the decline in the value of _____ assets over time. It is most commonly calculated by spreading the ________ cost of a fixed asset over its expected useful ____________, taking into account the scrap (or ________) value of the asset. This method of calculating depreciation is known as the __________ line method. For example, if a printing machine costs $10 000, has an expected residual value of $1000, and is depreciated over its expected 5-year lifespan, the annual depreciation amounts to ________. Some fixed assets, such as land and buildings, can increase in value over time (known as _____________), although they still incur costs, such as maintenance and repair.

Task 2: True or false?

		True/False
a.	Bank overdrafts and creditors are examples of current liabilities.	
b.	Capital expenditure can be interpreted from a balance sheet.	
c.	Cash flow forecasts are historical statements showing the cash movement of a business over time. This is shown by cash flow statements, not forecasts	
d.	In most countries, accountants and financial professionals must abide by the principles and ethics of accounting practices established by a regulatory body.	
e.	It is not a legal requirement for all companies to show all their shareholders the sources and uses of finance.	
f.	Net assets refers to the difference between a firm's total assets and its total liabilities.	
g.	Sole traders and partnerships are not required by law to publish their final accounts publically.	
h.	The profit figure shown in a profit and loss account is an accurate record that may be revised at a later date.	
i.	All fixed assets depreciate over a period of time. *(HL Only)*	
j.	Appreciation refers to an increase in the value of an asset over time. *(HL Only)*	
k.	Historic cost is the original price that a firm paid for the purchase of a fixed asset. *(HL Only)*	
l.	Motor vehicles tend to depreciate most in value at the beginning of their useful life. *(HL Only)*	
m.	The reducing-balance method of depreciation decreases the value of an asset by a fixed amount per time period. (HL Only)	

Task 3: Explain one …

a. Advantage of retaining a larger percentage of net profits (as retained profit) instead of allocating a greater amount to shareholders (as dividends).

b. Difference between net profit and gross profit.

c. Difficulty when comparing financial data between different businesses.

d. Reason for incorporated companies having to prepare and publish their final accounts.

e. Reason why a balance sheet must balance.

f. Difference between fixed and current assets.

g. Reason why assets might depreciate in value. *[HL Only]*

h. Way in which depreciation affects the profit and loss account. *[HL Only]*

i. Reason why motor vehicles are usually depreciated using the reducing-balance method rather than the straight-line method. *[HL Only]*

Task 4: Formulae

Identify the key term from its formula given below. *Hint*: answers appear in alphabetical order.

Formula	Key term
Opening stock + Purchases – Closing stock	
(Historic cost – Residual value) ÷ Lifespan of asset	
Net profit after interest and tax – Retained profit	
Sales revenue – Cost of goods sold	
Fixed assets + Working capital – Long term liabilities	
Gross profit – Expenses	
Net profit – Gross profit	
Total assets – Total liabilities	
Sales revenues – Total costs of production	
Net profit after interest and tax – Dividends	

Task 5: Calculations

a. Slater Tiling Company has an opening stock of $40,000, a closing stock of $25,000, and has purchased stock during the year costing $95 000. Calculate the firm's cost of goods sold (COGS).

b. Ortega Clothing Company has expenses of $345,000 and a net profit of $543,000. Calculate the firm's gross profit.

c. Tandy's Toys Ltd. purchases goods at $30,000 and manages to sell these for $68,000. State the:

i. Cost of goods sold

ii. Sales revenue

iii. Gross profit

d. Calculate the value of net profit from the following information for Mathieson Motors Co.:

- Sales turnover $250,000
- Cost of sales $100,000
- Expenses $55,000
- Interest payable $15,000

e. Complete the missing figures from the accounts of Heap Curtains Ltd.

Profit and loss account		Balance sheet	
	$		$
Sales turnover	800,000	Fixed assets	350,000
Cost of goods sold	450,000	Net current assets	250,000
Gross profit	i.	Long-term liabilities	180,000
Expenses	85,000	Net assets	iv.
Net profit	ii.	Retained profits	150,000
Interest and tax	53,000	Share capital	v.
Net profit after interest and tax	iii.	Equity	vi.

f. Pavlova Car Hire Co. bought a vehicle for $35,000 with an expected life of 4 years. Its residual value is estimated to be $7,000. Calculate the straight-line depreciation per year. *[HL Only]*

____

____

g. Assume that manufacturing equipment bought by Westmoreland Caterers cost $15,000 and has an expected useful life of 5 years. Annual depreciation is charged at 40%. Calculate the book value of the asset after two years. *[HL Only]*

____

____

Task 6: Multiple choice – Profit and loss

1. A business is not legally obliged to report which of the following?

A. Cash flow forecast

B. Cash flow statement

C. The balance sheet

D. The profit and loss account

2. What does the trading account gives details of?

A. Overheads and other costs of production

B. The cost of goods sold

C. The current value of the organization

D. The net profit (or loss) during a trading period

3. If expenses are greater than gross profit for a business, then the business

A. Can distribute a portion of the profits to shareholders

B. Has a positive net profit balance

C. Has made an overall loss

D. Has performed well on financial grounds

4. In which account would overheads and expenses appear?

A. Appropriation account

B. Balance sheet

C. Profit and loss account

D. Trading account

5. The profit and loss account

   A. Calculates the gross profit of a business

   B. Lists all revenue and expenditure of a business over a trading period

   C. Shows all assets of a business during a trading period

   D. Shows the amount of money owed to other businesses

6. Which of the following items does not appear in a profit and loss account?

   A. Cost of goods sold

   B. Expenses

   C. Machinery and equipment

   D. Overheads

7. On a profit and loss account, dividends represent

   A. The numerical difference between retained profit and expenses

   B. The numerical difference between tax and interest payments

   C. The portion of net profits after interest and tax that is distributed to shareholders

   D. The portion of net profits that is reinvested by the business

8. The appropriation account does not show

   A. Corporate tax

   B. Dividends

   C. Interest charges

   D. Retained profits

9. Which of the following cannot be applied to gross profit?

   A. Appears on the trading account

   B. Calculated as sales revenue minus the cost of goods sold

   C. Calculated by total revenue minus the cost of sales

   D. Expressed as a percentage to allow for historical and inter-firm comparisons

10. Expenses are the

    A. Costs of non-trading activities

    B. Direct costs of trading activities

    C. Direct costs of non-trading activities

    D. Indirect costs of trading activities

11. Expenses do not include

A. Cost of sales

B. Depreciation

C. Insurance premiums

D. Rent

12. Calculate the cost of sales from the following information:

- Cost of stock per unit = $20
- Units of stock purchases = 800
- Closing stock = 300 units
- Opening stock = 250 units

A. $5,000

B. $15,000

C. $22,000

D. $27,000

Questions 13–15 refer to the following information.

- Cost of sales $35,000
- Expenses $25,000
- Retained profit $20,000
- Tax $15,000
- Sales turnover $110,000

13. What is the firm's gross profit?

A. $35,000

B. $50,000

C. $55,000

D. $75,000

14. What is the firm's net profit?

A. $75,000

B. $70,000

C. $55,000

D. $50,000

15. What is the firm's total dividend payout to shareholders?

A. $5,000

B. $10,000

C. $15,000

D. $20,000

16. Ekunda Grocers earns $200,000 in sales, has expenses of $80,000 and cost of goods sold amount to $90,000. What is the firm's gross profit?

A. $30,000

B. $110,000

C. $120,000

D. $170,000

17. Which of the following is not be classed as an expense in the profit and loss account?

A. Direct costs

B. Fixed costs

C. Indirect costs

D. Rent and administration

18. Use the following information to work out the net profit before tax:

- Cost of sales $50,000
- Expenses $30,000
- Interest payable $1,000
- Sales turnover $100,000

A. $19,000

B. $20,000

C. $49,000

D. $50,000

19. Interest payable means

A. Interest imposed on debtors for late payment

B. Interest paid to debenture holders

C. Interest paid to financial lenders

D. Interest received from cash deposits at the bank

20. A firm can increase its gross profit by

A. All of the below

B. Cutting advertising expenditure

C. Reducing management salaries

D. Using cheaper suppliers

Task 7: Multiple choice – Balance sheet

1. The publication of final accounts includes the following, except for the

   A. Cash flow forecast

   B. Cash flow statement

   C. The balance sheet

   D. The profit and loss account

2. The main purpose of constructing a balance sheet is to

   A. Allow stakeholders and investors to assess a firm's liquidity

   B. Identify the correct amount of tax liability based on the value of the business

   C. Provide financial data and information for shareholders

   D. Show the value of a business at a particular point in time

3. Suppliers would be interested in the final accounts of a business in order to

   A. Assess business profitability and performance

   B. Calculate corporate tax liabilities

   C. Negotiate pay and productivity agreements

   D. Secure external sources of finance

4. In which final account would you find shareholders' funds?

   A. Balance sheet

   B. Cash flow forecast

   C. Profit and loss account

   D. Trading account

5. Which of the following items is not found in a balance sheet?

   A. Intangible fixed assets

   B. Liabilities falling due after one year

   C. Net profits before interest and tax

   D. Trade creditors

6. Which item appears on the balance sheet of a sole trader?

   A. Capital and reserves

   B. Debentures

   C. Owner's equity

   D. Shareholders' funds

7. Money owed to other people or organizations is shown in a balance sheet as

   A. Current liabilities

   B. Debts

   C. Liabilities

   D. Net Assets

8. Which of the following is not considered to be a fixed asset?

   A. Debtors

   B. Fixed capital

   C. Land

   D. Trademarks

9. Fixed assets include all the following except

   A. Finished goods for sale

   B. Intangible assets

   C. Investment expenditure

   D. Physical assets

10. Current assets do not include

    A. Creditors

    B. Debtors

    C. Inventories

    D. Work-in-progress

11. Which of the following is most likely to be a long-term business liability?

    A. Debentures

    B. Hire purchase

    C. Loans

    D. Overdraft

12. Which of the following is not a current liability?

    A. Creditors

    B. Debtors

    C. Dividends

    D. Tax

13. Which of the following does not usually apply to fixed assets?

- **A.** Assets owned by a business for more than 12 months
- **B.** Assets that a business intends to keep for more than 12 months
- **C.** Assets that generate cash sales for a firm
- **D.** Intangible assets such as brands, logos and slogans

14. If a firm buys a delivery vehicle with cash, how will this be reflected in the balance sheet?

- **A.** An increase in depreciation charges and a fall in the cash balance
- **B.** An increase in the net cash outflow
- **C.** An increase in the value of fixed assets with a corresponding fall in the value of cash
- **D.** An increase in the value of net assets

15. Which statement about tangible assets is true?

- **A.** Assets that are not always possible to value, such as brands
- **B.** Assets that depreciate in value over time
- **C.** They are physical assets owned by the firm for long term use
- **D.** They represent the use of funds of a business

16. A patent

- **A.** Gives the exclusive rights to the use of a brand name, symbol or slogan
- **B.** Is a type of physical fixed asset that does not necessarily appear on a balance sheet
- **C.** Provides legal protection against those copying the printed work of others
- **D.** Provides legal protection for an inventor to prevent others from copying it

17. Which of the following is not an intangible asset?

- **A.** Cash deposits at the bank
- **B.** Copyrights and trademarks
- **C.** Goodwill
- **D.** Investments

18. Which statement cannot be applied to goodwill?

- **A.** It can only be truly measured once a business is sold at a premium to its book value
- **B.** It includes the value of labour such as their market value if they were headhunted
- **C.** It is a type of intangible fixed asset
- **D.** It is a value of the firm's customer and staff loyalty

19. Intangible assets are

A. Current assets that add value to a business

B. Non-physical fixed assets of a business

C. Physical fixed assets that add value to a business

D. Services that add value to a business

20. Intangible assets include all the following, except

A. Brand names

B. Goodwill

C. Services

D. Trademarks

21. Net assets is calculated by which formula?

A. Fixed assets + Current assets

B. Fixed assets + Current assets – Current liabilities

C. Fixed assets + Working capital

D. Fixed assets + Working capital – Long-term liabilities

22. Which of the following equations is found in a balance sheet of a public limited company?

A. Equity = Current liabilities + working capital – long term liabilities

B. Net assets = Share capital + retained profit

C. Net current assets = Liabilities + shareholders' funds + retained profit

D. Total assets = Total liabilities

23. Owners' equity does not include the calculation of

A. Fixed assets

B. Ordinary share capital

C. Retained profit

D. Shareholders' funds

24. Which of the following is not considered as a guiding principle to accounting practices?

A. Bureaucracy

B. Confidentiality

C. Integrity

D. Objectivity

25. Calculate the value of net current assets from the following information.

- Land = $50,000
- Creditors = $10,000
- Share capital = $200,000
- Cash = $10,000
- Stock = $20,000
- Overdrafts = $25,000
- Loans = $30,000

A. ($5,000)

B. $30,000

C. $200,000

D. $215,000

26. Suppose a firm has opening stock of $5000, purchases of $6000 and cost of goods sold valued at $8000. What is the value of its closing stock?

A. $3,000

B. $7,000

C. $9,000

D. $19,000

27. Physical assets tend to depreciate over time. Which asset below does not generally follow this trend? *[HL Only]*

A. Brands

B. Cash

C. Land

D. Machinery

28. An increase in the value of certain fixed assets, such as land and buildings, is known as [HL Only]

A. Advances

B. Appreciation

C. Depreciation

D. Enlargement

Questions 29 and 30 refer to the following information.

Barragan Consultancy uses the declining balance method to depreciate its fixed assets. The firm purchases computers worth $300,000 and uses a depreciation rate of 30%. The computers are expected to last 5 years before being replaced.

29. What is the net book value of the computers after two years? *[HL Only]*

A. $90,000

B. $120,000

C. $147,000

D. $180,000

30. What would the annual depreciation charge be if Barragan Consultancy had used the straight line depreciation method for the computers? *[HL Only]*

A. $60,000

B. $90,000

C. $120,000

D. $300,000

Unit 3.5 Profitability and ratio analysis

Task 1: Complete the missing words

Ratio analysis is useful for anyone who has a direct __________________ in the financial performance of a business. These people or organizations are known as the __________________ of the business, such as:

- __________________ – These people or organizations are interested in the return on their ______________ so will be interested in financial ratios related to the firm's profitability.
- __________________ – The personnel are interested in the profitability of the organization because this will influence their ______________ and job security.
- __________________ – The leadership team are interested in the firm's financial ratios in order to gauge performance and to aid ______________ -making.
- __________________ – These stakeholders are interested in the ______________ position of the business because this affects the firm's ability to pay for their goods and services.
- __________________ – Banks, for instance, are interested in the long term liquidity position of a business in order to judge its ability to repay ______________ .
- __________________ – Rival firms are interested in gauging the performance of the business. This is often used as part of their benchmarking practice.
- __________________ – The state (authorities) look at the financial performance of a business to ensure that proper accounting procedures are followed (to prevent fraudulent reporting of finances) and to calculate the correct amount of ______________ owed by the firm.

Task 2: Explain …

Explain the error(s) made in each of the following definitions of return on capital employed (ROCE):

a. "ROCE is the profit expressed as a return on capital employed".

____

____

____

b. "ROCE is profit made that is greater than capital spent".

____

____

____

c. "ROCE is profit that covers all your set-up costs".

____

____

____

____

d. "ROCE shows the amount of profit that a firm makes".

Task 3: Vocabulary quiz

Identify the key terms from the clues given. *Hint*: the answers are in reverse alphabetical order!

Key term	Definition
	This important ratio measures a firm's efficiency and profitability in relation to its size (as measured by the capital employed).
	Also known as the acid-test ratio, this liquidity ratio measures a firm's ability to meet its short-term debts. It ignores stock because some inventories are hard to turn into cash in a short time frame.
	Ratios that look at the level and value of a firm's profits.
	Measures overall profit (after all costs have been deducted) as a percentage of sales revenue.
	Ratios that look at a firm's ability to pay its debts.
	This profitability ratio shows gross profit expressed as a percentage of sales revenue.
	This short term liquidity ratio calculates the ability of a firm to meet its debts within the next twelve months.
	The value of all long term sources of finance for a business, e.g. bank loans, share capital and accumulated retained profits.
	Liquidity ratio that measures a firm's ability to meet its short-term debts. It ignores stocks as not all inventories can be easily turned into cash.

Task 4: Complete the table

Use the information given in the table below to identify the ratio and the type of ratio (profitability, liquidity or efficiency).

Formula	Ratio	Type of Ratio
(Current assets – Stock) ÷ Current liabilities		
(Gross profit ÷ Sales revenue) × 100		
(Net profit ÷ Capital Employed) × 100		
(Net profit ÷ Sales revenue) × 100		
Current assets ÷ Current liabilities		

Task 5: True or false?

		True/False
a.	A firm that has a long working capital cycle will tend to use the acid test ratio to measure its liquidity.	
b.	A liquidity crisis exists when a business is unable to pay its short-term debts.	
c.	Capital employed is the sum of equity capital, accumulated retained profit and long term liabilities.	
e.	Profitability ratios are used to see the amount of profits earned by a business.	
f.	Profitable firms that lack sufficient liquidity are unlikely to survive in the long run.	
g.	Ratio analysis is a quantitative management tool for analysing and judging the financial performance of a business.	
h.	Shareholders are more concerned about dividend earnings than capital growth.	
i.	The higher the net profit margin, the greater the financial return as a percentage of the firm's sales revenue.	
j.	The ROCE ratio can be improved by strategies that increase the level of a firm's sales revenues.	
k.	When the value of a firm's stock (inventory) increases, the acid test ratio will fall.	

Task 6: Multiple choice

1. Which of the following is not a financial performance ratio?

A. Acid test ratio

B. Labour turnover rate

C. Net profit margin

D. Return on capital employed

2. Calculating the return on capital employed (ROCE) provides information on a firm's

A. Effectiveness in its use of capital resources

B. Financial return to potential investors and shareholders

C. Liquidity (or solvency)

D. Profitability position

3. Which ratio would a business prefer not to be very high in value?

A. Current test

B. Gross profit margin

C. Net profit margin

D. Return on capital employed

4. The acid test ratio can be used to identify a firm's

   A. Ability to pay its long term liabilities

   B. Ability to pay its short term debts

   C. Financial return on the use of fixed assets

   D. Profitability position

5. The net profit margin can be used to identify a firm's

   A. Ability to control its overheads

   B. Ability to pay its debts

   C. Amount of return to its shareholders

   D. Profitability position

6. If a firm has gross profit of $3 million, sales revenue of $5 million and expenses of $1 million, then the net profit margin would be

   A. 40%

   B. 60%

   C. $1 million

   D. $2 million

7. The ratio that measures a firm's profit in relation to its size is called the

   A. Gross profit margin

   B. Net profit before interest and tax

   C. Net profit margin

   D. Return on capital employed

8. If a business has gross profit of $100 million, overheads of $10 million and capital employed of $200 million, then its return on capital employed is

   A. 45%

   B. 50%

   C. 55%

   D. 220%

9. Firm A has net profit of $135 million from its capital employed of $300m. Firm B has net profit of $175 million from its capital employed of $420 million. Which firm has the better efficiency ratio?

   A. Firm A as its ROCE is 45% compared to Firm B's ROCE ratio of less than 42%

   B. Firm B, as its profit is almost 30% higher than that of Firm A

   C. Firm B, as its ROCE is 45% compared to Firm A's ROCE ratio of less than 42%

   D. Firm B, as it has earned $40m more than Firm A

10. Calculate the current ratio using the following information for a business:

- cash = $100,000
- debtors = $60,000
- stocks = $140,000
- overdrafts = $50,000
- trade creditors = $70,000

A. 40%

B. 250%

C. 2.5:1

D. $180 000

11. Capital employed is equal to

A. Assets employed minus long-term liabilities

B. Net assets minus liabilities

C. Shareholders' funds minus long-term liabilities

D. Shareholders' funds plus long-term liabilities

12. Which of the following ratios can be 'too high' (undesirable) from a firm's point of view?

A. Gross profit margin

B. Net profit margin

C. Return on capital employed

D. The current ratio

13. The ability of a firm to pay its short-term debts without having to sell any of its stock (inventory) is shown by which ratio?

A. Current ratio

B. Efficiency ratio

C. Liquidity ratio

D. Quick ratio

14. Ratio analysis cannot address which question below?

A. Can the firm pay its liabilities?

B. Has the firm's market share improved?

C. How does the firm's performance compare to its nearest rivals?

D. How profitable is the business?

15. Which option below is not a reason for conducting financial ratio analysis?

A. Best practice benchmarking

B. To aid management decision-making and control

C. To calculate the value of net profit over time

D. To improve organizational accountability

Unit 3.6 Efficiency ratio analysis *[HL Only]*

Task 1: True or false?

		True/False
a.	A highly geared firm is generally vulnerable to changes in interest rates.	
b.	A highly geared firm is more at risk during an economic recession.	
c.	Efficiency ratios show how well an organization's resources have been used to generate profit from the available capital of the business.	
d.	It is considered too risky to invest in a firm with a gearing ratio of 50% or above.	
e.	Profits tend to be more volatile in businesses with high gearing.	
f.	Highly geared firms are seen as being a risky investment as they are unlikely to make much profit.	
g.	The creditor days ratio is measured by using the formula (Creditors ÷ Cost of Sales) × 365.	
h.	The stock turnover ratio is measured using the formula Stock ÷ Cost of sales. Other way round, i.e. Cost of sales ÷ Stock	
i.	When the value of creditors rise, the creditor days ratio will rise.	
j.	The debtor days ratio is measured by the formula (Debtors ÷ sales revenue) × 365	
k.	The creditor days ratio measures the number of days it takes, on average, for a business to pay its lenders (financiers).	
l.	Efficiency ratios look at how well a firm uses its resources.	

Task 2: Explain …

a. Whether the creditor days ratio should, ideally, be high or low.

____

____

____

____

b. Whether the stock turnover rate should, ideally, be high or low.

____

____

____

____

HIGHER LEVEL

c. Whether the gearing ratio should be high or low. *Hint*: 'it depends'.

d. Whether the debtor days ratio should, ideally, be high or low.

e. How high gearing might be profitable for some businesses.

f. Which company represents the higher risk to potential investors, given the limited amount of data.

	JJ Clothing Ltd	LL Clothing Ltd
Capital employed	$1 000 000	$1 100 000
Debentures	$100 000	$150 000
Mortgage	$350 000	$280 000

g. Why highly geared firms are more exposed to the pressures of an economic downturn (recession).

Task 3: Multiple choice

1. Which of the following is not a short-term liquidity ratio?
   - **A.** Acid test
   - **B.** Current
   - **C.** Gearing
   - **D.** Quick

2. What does the gearing ratio measure?
   - **A.** The borrowing of a firm as a percentage of its total assets
   - **B.** The proportion of the a firm's capital employed formed by interest-bearing debt
   - **C.** The value of a firm's long term finances
   - **D.** The value of creditors in relation to a firm's capital employed

3. Gearing can be calculated as
   - **A.** External sources of finance as a percentage of the total assets employed
   - **B.** Liabilities as a percentage of the capital employed
   - **C.** Loan capital plus other borrowings expressed as a proportion of the capital employed
   - **D.** Net assets minus long-term liabilities

4. Which statement below cannot be applied to the gearing ratio?
   - **A.** Creditors prefer firms to have high gearing as it means they make more profit
   - **B.** Firms with a high gearing ratio are generally considered to be a risky investment
   - **C.** It is a long term liquidity ratio
   - **D.** It uses the amount of external sources of finance as part of the calculation

5. Which of the following sources of finance will increase the value of the gearing ratio?
   - **A.** Bank overdraft
   - **B.** Debentures
   - **C.** Debt factoring
   - **D.** Share issue

6. The gearing ratio calculated by using which formula?
   - **A.** (Liabilities ÷ Capital employed) × 100
   - **B.** (Long-term liabilities ÷ Equity finance plus long-term liabilities) × 100
   - **C.** (Long-term liabilities ÷ Sales revenue) × 100
   - **D.** (Short-term liabilities + Long-term liabilities) ÷ capital employed

HIGHER LEVEL

7. It is generally desirable for a firm to have a relatively low value for which of its financial ratios?

   A. Debtor days

   B. Gross profit margin

   C. Net profit margin

   D. Stock turnover rate

8. The debtor days ratio shows

   A. Credit sales as a percentage of sales turnover

   B. How long it takes, on average, for a firm to collect its debts from customers

   C. How long it takes, on average, for a firm to pay its debts to suppliers and creditors

   D. The value of debtors as a percentage of sales turnover

9. The creditor days ratio shows

   A. Credit sales as a percentage of sales turnover

   B. How long it takes, on average, for a firm to collect its debts from customers

   C. How long it takes, on average, for a firm to pay its debts to suppliers and creditors

   D. The value of creditors as a percentage of sales turnover

10. Suppose Paisey Ltd. has sales revenues of $150,000, cost of sales valued at $70,000 and debtors to the value of $30,000. What is the average debt collection period for the firm?

   A. 27 days

   B. 73 days

   C. 97 days

   D. 243 days

11. Which business would be least pleased with a stock turnover ratio of 95 days?

   A. Boeing (aircraft manufacturer)

   B. Honda Motor Company (cars)

   C. McDonald's (fast food restaurants)

   D. Reebok (sports apparel)

12. A business is most likely to prefer a ______ debt collection period with a ________ creditor days ratio.

   A. Long, Large

   B. Long, Small

   C. Short, Large

   D. Short, Small

13. What does the stock turnover ratio measure?

A. How much stock is purchased per time period

B. Sales revenue as a percentage of the average stock level

C. The level of stock compared with the sales turnover

D. The number of times a business sells its stocks in a given time period

14. If Wenger Inc. has sold stock valued at a cost of $150,000 (the cost of sales) and owes $36,000 to trade creditors, what is the creditor days ratio?

A. 6 days

B. 17 days

C. 61 days

D. 83 days

15. Which statement below cannot be applied to short-term liquidity ratios?

A. They compare the ratio of current assets to current liabilities

B. They involve calculating the ability of firms to pay their short-term debts

C. They look at the level of gearing within firms

D. They measure the ability of businesses to meet their short term liabilities

Unit 3.7 Cash flow

Task 1: Vocabulary quiz

Identify the key terms from the clues given. *Hint*: the answers are in alphabetical order.

Key term	Definition
	The most liquid of current assets, this is the actual money a business has, either in hand or at the bank.
	Quantitative technique used to predict how cash is likely to flow into and out of a business in the foreseeable future.
	Short-term assets of an organization that can be converted into cash within a year, e.g. stocks, debtors and cash.
	Money owed to creditors and financiers that is repayable within the next twelve months.
	People or other organizations that owe money to the business as they have purchased goods on credit. This is a category of current assets.
	This dilemma is caused by a lack of cash because the firm's net cash flow is negative.
	This is calculated by using the formula cash inflow minus cash outflow per time period .
	A financial service that allow pre-approved customers to temporarily take out more money than the amount available in their bank account.
	The yield (return) that is calculated by subtracting total costs from total revenues.
	Also known as 'net current assets', this is cash or liquid assets available for the daily running of a business.

Task 2: Outline ...

a. Two reasons why a new restaurant is likely to have poor cash flow in its first few months of operation.

____

____

____

____

b. Three different ways that a business might be able to improve its cash flow position.

____

____

____

____

c. The difference between sales revenue and profits.

____

____

____

____

d. Why debtors are considered to be an asset.

e. Two major causes of cash flow crises for a business.

f. Two ways that a hotel might be able to improve its net cash flow.

Task 3: Explain the difference between …

a. A cash flow statement and a cash flow forecast.

b. Debtors and creditors.

c. Current assets and fixed assets.

d. Cash and profit.

____

____

____

____

Task 4: True or false?

		True/False
a.	A cash flow forecast is used to show the final profit in a trading period.	
b.	A cash flow statement records the cash streams in and out of a business over the past year.	
c.	A highly geared firm has a large percentage of interest-bearing capital.	
d.	Negotiating shorter payment periods with creditors helps to improve cash flow.	
e.	Net current assets is another term for working capital.	
f.	Profit is more important than cash to a business.	
g.	The higher the liquidity of an asset, the easier and quicker it is to turn it into cash.	
h.	There is a positive correlation between cash flow and profit.	
i.	Tight credit control is vital if a business wants to avoid cash flow problems.	
j.	Without stocks (inventory), a business would not be able to survive for very long.	
k.	Working capital can be negative, but only in the short term.	
l.	Working capital is the cash that a firm has for its day-to-day running.	

Task 5: Crossword

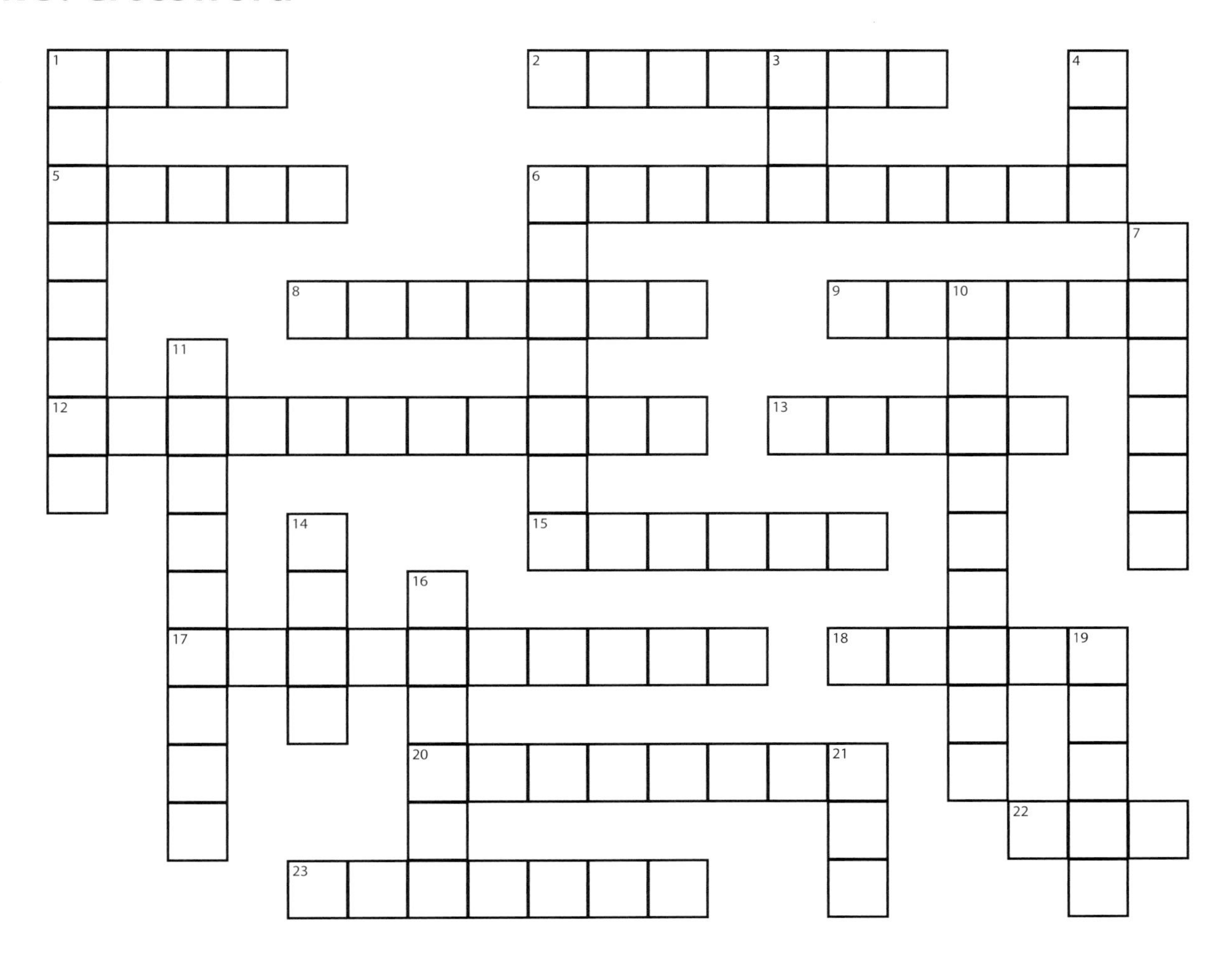

Clues across

1. The most liquid of all assets (4)
2. The situation when cash inflow equals cash outflow (7)
5. Another term for revenue or turnover (5)
6. Another term for closing balance – ____ cash flow (10)
8. Firms or people who owe money to another firm (7)
9. Part of a firm's liquid assets (6)
12. Occurs if a business attempts to expand too rapidly, without a sufficient financial base (11)
13. One of the largest outflows for most businesses (5)
15. Firms that are highly _______ have to pay out a lot in interest payments (6)
17. What a firm faces in extreme and prolonged cases of cash flow problems (10)
18. A possible interest-bearing solution to resolving a cash flow deficit, offered by banks (5)
20. To predict the cash flows of a business (8)
22. Cash inflow minus cash outflow = ____ cash flow (3)
23. Cash leaving a firm (7)

Clues down

1. Refers to the money flowing into and out of a business (4,4)
3. Value of the closing balance when opening balance + receipts = payments (3)
4. Debt factoring service providers will insist on charging this (3)
6. Cash balance at the end of the month (7)
7. These could be sold to raise cash (6)
10. Service that allows a business to withdraw more money than exists in its account (9)
11. Sale and _______ – a method of improving cash flow for firms with liquidity issues (9)
14. Banks do this to help firms with a cash flow problem, for a fee of course (4)
16. Do not confuse this surplus with cash (6)
19. Another name for revenue ______ (5)
21. Business rates, as a compulsory levy, are an example of this type of cash outflow (3)

Task 6: Multiple choice

1. Which statement below does not apply to the components of capital in an incorporated company?

   A. Accumulated retained profits

   B. Cash used to buy current assets

   C. Long-term bank loans

   D. Share capital

2. Which of the following is a current liability?

   A. Cash

   B. Debentures

   C. Overdrafts

   D. Stocks

3. What are debtors?

   A. Businesses that have sold items and are awaiting cash payment

   B. Customers who have bought products but did not pay for them in cash

   C. Individuals or businesses in debt

   D. People or businesses that have sold items on credit

4. Currents assets do not include

   A. Copyright and patents

   B. Raw materials

   C. Unfinished goods

   D. Unsold finished goods

5. The legal responsibility of a business for the money it owes to other parties due in more than 12 months' time is called

   A. External financing

   B. Long-term liabilities

   C. Long-term loans

   D. Security (or collateral)

6. Which of the following is not a current liability?

   A. Corporate tax

   B. Interest charges

   C. Trade creditors

   D. Work-in-progress

7. Which of the following would not be classed as a current asset?

   A. Cash at the bank

   B. Debtors

   C. Stocks (inventories)

   D. Trade creditors

8. Which of the following is a fixed asset?

   A. Cash in hand

   B. Fixtures and fittings

   C. Raw materials

   D. Work-in-progress

9. The majority of stock held by a retailer will be in the form of

   A. Cash

   B. Finished goods

   C. Working capital

   D. Work-in-progress

10. Working capital can be defined as

    A. The difference between a firm's total assets and its total liabilities

    B. The difference between the assets and liabilities of a business

    C. The money that is available for the daily operations of a business

    D. The value of the money that belongs to a business

11. How is working capital calculated?

    A. Cash inflow less Cash outflows

    B. Current assets less Current liabilities

    C. Net assets less Net liabilities

    D. Opening balance plus Net cash flow

12. Hanley Sports Equipment predicts a closing year-end balance of $50,000. The firm later discovers that an order for $8,000 was ignored from the sales figure and that a utility bill for $3,000 was unpaid. What should the new closing balance be?

    A. $3,000

    B. $39,000

    C. $55,000

    D. $61,000

13. What is the net cash flow for K. Reed & Co, given the following financial information?

K. Reed & Co. Annual Cash Flow Statement (excerpts):

- Opening balance: $35,000
- Cash inflow: $95,000
- Cash outflow: $50,000

A. $45,000

B. $75,000

C. $80,000

D. $110,000

14. What would a contingency fund be used for?

A. To entice customers to pay by cash rather than on credit

B. To fund business growth

C. To improve liquidity during unforeseen events

D. To pay suppliers and other creditors

15. Which of the following is not a sign of a business that is overtrading?

A. A fall in the value of trade debtors

B. An increase in liquidity problems

C. Higher than usual amounts of work-in-progress

D. Higher than usual levels of finished goods

16. The financial document that shows how cash has flowed into a business and what it has spent the cash on is known as the

A. Cash flow forecast

B. Cash flow statement

C. Profit and loss account

D. Sales budget

17. In the worst case scenario, what can firms sell if they are struggling to survive?

A. Certain fixed assets

B. Debentures

C. Some net assets

D. Venture capital

18. One major purpose of constructing a cash flow forecast is to

A. Identify the sources of cash inflows and cash outflows

B. Present information on the sources of sales revenues and costs of production

C. Provide a planning and decision-making tool for managing a firm's cash flows

D. Show the value of profit made by a firm at the end of each trading session

19. Causes of cash flow crises are not likely to include

A. High gearing

B. Money tied up in stocks and inventory

C. Overtrading

D. Tight credit control

20. Which of the following is most likely to improve a firm's cash flow position?

A. Greater value of debtors

B. Higher interest rates

C. Longer credit periods

D. Using hire-purchase

Unit 3.8 Investment appraisal

Task 1: Complete the missing words

Investment is the ______________ used to increase the productive capacity and operations of a business. It includes the purchase of ______________ assets, such as buildings, equipment, machinery and motor vehicles.

The ___________ ___________ (PBP) method of investment appraisal measures the length of time it takes for an investment project to generate enough ______________ to recoup the investment cost. It is quick to calculate but does not tend to favour ________ - ___________ projects, i.e. those with a long payback period.

The ___________ rate of return (ARR) measures the annual profit generated from an investment project, expressed as a _______________ of the investment cost. The ______________the ARR, the better the return from the investment.

[HL Only]

_______ _______ _______ (NPV) considers the opportunity cost of money because money received in the future is worth _______than it is worth if it were received today. _______ _______ _______ (DCF) are used to express the ___________ value of money. In general, an investment project is financially feasible if its NPV is ____________.

Task 2: Outline the relationship between …

a. Contribution and payback period.

____

____

____

b. Interest rates for savings and the average rate of return.

____

____

____

c. Interest rate charges and the level of gearing.

____

____

____

d. Time and discounted factors *[HL Only]*.

____

____

____

e. The discount rate and the net present value *[HL Only]*.

____

____

____

____

Task 3: True or false?

		True/False
a.	Bad debts occur when debtors are unable to pay their bills.	
b.	Considering the future value of money, the higher the interest rate, the less money is worth if received in the future.	
c.	Investment appraisal is a forward-looking decision making tool.	
d.	Payback period uses the flow of profits to assess the feasibility of an investment.	
e.	Profit is the value of sales revenue after all costs have been accounted for.	
f.	Sales revenue is the value of goods and/or services sold to customers,	
g.	The higher the value of the average rate of return, the more financially feasible an investment project tends to be.	
h.	Working capital is also known as net current assets.	
i.	Discounting is important to account for the future value of cash flows. (HL Only)	
j.	The accounting rate of return and the net present value methods of investment appraisal are expressed in percentage terms. (HL Only)	
k.	The net present value is relatively easier to calculate than the payback period. (HL Only)	

Task 4: Vocabulary quiz

Identify the key terms from the clues given. *Hint*: the answers are in alphabetical order.

Key term	Definition
	An investment appraisal technique that calculates the typical annual profit of an investment project, expressed as a percentage of the initial sum of the money invested.
	A technique that reduces the value of the money a business receives in future years. Money loses its value over time, so this tool is applied to give money a current (present-day) value for the expected future returns.
	The spending on fixed assets with the potential to yield future financial benefits, e.g. upgrading computer equipment or the purchase of a building.
	An investment appraisal technique that calculates the total discounted cash flows, minus the initial cost of an investment project. If this figure is positive, then the investment is viable on financial grounds.
	This is an investment appraisal technique which estimates the length of time that it will take to recoup the initial cash outflow of an investment project.
	The original amount of money (or historic cost) invested in a particular project.
	Non-quantitative techniques used to judge whether an investment project is worthwhile, such as whether an investment decision is compatible with the organizational culture.

Task 5: Multiple choice

1. Which of the following is an example of investment in a business context?

   A. Borrowing money from a bank

   B. Paying dividends to shareholders

   C. Purchasing new machinery

   D. Saving money in a bank

2. Factors that affect a multinational company's investment decision are least likely to include

   A. Leadership and management styles

   B. Oorganizational objectives

   C. The impact on human relations

   D. Unquantifiable risks

3. Which of the following investment appraisal techniques uses time as its unit of measurement?

   A. Average rate of return

   B. Discounted cash flows

   C. Net present value

   D. Payback period

4. Which investment appraisal method allows a firm to see whether it will break-even on the purchase of a fixed asset before it needs to be replaced?

   A. Average rate of return

   B. Discounted cash flows

   C. Net present value

   D. Payback period

5. The average rate of return can best be described as an investment appraisal technique that

   A. Calculates the average annual profit of a project as a percentage of the principal

   B. Calculates the total profit of a project as a percentage of the initial investment cost

   C. Measures the accounting period for which a project will break-even and earn a profit

   D. Measures the future value of net cash flows for an investment project

6. Which quantitative factor applies to a firm considering investing in a new computerized stock control system?

   A. Consideration of upgradeability and compatibility with future technologies

   B. Staff training concerns and issues

   C. The firm's cash flow position

   D. Time to implement the new computerized system

7. Which of the following is least important for firms that use the payback period method of investment appraisal?

   A. Firms seeking a quick return on their investment
   B. Firms that focus on profitability rather than short term cash flows
   C. Firms that focus on time as a priority
   D. Firms that see liquidity as more important than profitability

8. Which statement below does not apply to the payback period?

   A. It favours projects that have high profitability over time
   B. It is simpler to calculate and understand than other investment appraisal methods
   C. The timing of net cash flows is largely ignored
   D. Time, rather than profit, is the focus of attention

9. Which business situation would most suit the payback method of investment appraisal?

   A. A new multi-complex cinema and entertainment centre
   B. Firms that can afford to use cash to raise the necessary finance for investment
   C. Manufacturing processes where technology changes frequently
   D. The building of a new international airport

10. The payback period is least favourable as a measure of investment appraisal when

   A. The costs of investment need to be regained quickly
   B. Firms have a poor cash flow position
   C. Projects are expected to return a profit in the medium to long term
   D. Time is a major priority

11. Qualitative factors to consider in an investment appraisal do not include

   A. Alternative investment projects and their potential yields (returns)
   B. External factors such as the state of technology
   C. The aims and objectives of the business
   D. The organizational culture, such as the degree of employee participation

12. Which limitation applies specifically to the average rate of return?

   A. It does not consider quantitative factors
   B. It favours only short term investment projects
   C. It focuses on time rather than profit
   D. It ignores the timing and pattern of cash flow

13. Which of the following is not a qualitative factor affecting investment appraisal?

A. Expected changes in interest rates, thereby affecting the real value of money

B. New competing products being launched by rival firms

C. The state of the economy, such as the rate of inflation and unemployment

D. Uncertainties about the future

14. The net present value of an investment helps to establish the value of _________ flows of income and expenditure. The _________ the numerical value of the discount factor, the lower the value of future cash flows in real terms. *[HL Only]*

A. Future, Higher

B. Future, Lower

C. Present, Higher

D. Present, Lower

15. Which investment appraisal method is not a measure of profit or profitability? [HL Only]

A. Average rate of return

B. Discounted cash flows

C. Net present values

D. Payback period

16. If interest rates are 5% per annum, what is the present value of $100 received next year? *[HL Only]*

A. $95.00

B. $95.24

C. $96.45

D. $105.00

17. Which term below refers to the number used to work out the present value of a sum of money received in the future? *[HL Only]*

A. Discount factor

B. Discounted cash flows

C. Net cash flow

D. Net present value

18. Which of the following is not a quantitative investment appraisal technique? [HL Only]

A. Average rate of return

B. Discounted cash flows

C. Payback period

D. Variance analysis

19. Limitations of the net present value method of investment appraisal do not include *[HL Only]*

A. Changes in interest rates will alter the NPV figure

B. It accounts for medium to long term projects

C. NPV can be tedious to calculate

D. The difficulty of forecasting cash flows in the distant future

20. Which statement does not apply to the use of net present values? *[HL Only]*

A. A positive NPV means that the investment decision is justifiable on financial grounds

B. It relies on the use of discounted cash flows

C. The NPV is expressed in percentage terms to allow for easier benchmarking

D. The NPV value will fall if interest rates rise

Unit 3.9 Budgets *[HL Only]*

HIGHER LEVEL

Task 1: Complete the missing words

____________ refers to the art of financial control in an organization. A __________ is a financial plan that an organization strives to achieve as it allows the firm to check its progress against the budgeted (planned) targets. A budget should reflect the _______ of an organization, e.g. if the firm plans to replace expensive capital equipment, then the amount should be incorporated into the budget. Budgets can be used for any quantitative variable, e.g. _______ revenue, costs, profit, staffing, advertising expenditure and capital __________ on fixed assets.

In reality, it is likely that there will be deviations from the budget plan. __________ analysis is a management tool used to calculate differences in the actual and __________ figures. A __________ variance occurs when the _______ outcome is better than the budgeted (planned) outcome. By contrast, an ___________ variance occurs when the actual outcome is ________ than the budgeted plan. The analysis also looks at the reasons for the differences that occur and can therefore be a useful analytical tool in assessing the success of a strategy.

Managing the finances of a business becomes more difficult as a business grows in size. Costs and ___________ from different areas of the business become harder to account for. Hence, cost centres and/or profit centres are established, with a manager being held responsible for the costs and/or revenues incurred for each department (or centre). All _______ centres are also _________ centres, but ________ centres are not necessarily _______ centres.

Task 2: True or false?

		True/False
a.	A favourable variance exists when the difference between the budgeted and actual outcome is financially beneficial.	
b.	Budgeting ignores qualitative factors that affect the financial performance of an organization.	
c.	Budgeting is more difficult for businesses with seasonal fluctuations in demand and where costs are harder to predict.	
d.	Budgets are backwards-looking as they are based on past trends, such as last year's budgeted sales figures.	
e.	Budgets can be inaccurate due to unforeseen changes that can cause large differences between the budgeted figures and the actual outcomes.	
f.	Budgets help businesses to have better financial control.	
g.	It is more useful for budgeting to have profit centres in an organization than it is to have cost centres.	
h.	Organizations that have an open and entrusting corporate culture tend to use budgets as a form of empowerment and motivation.	

Task 3: Vocabulary quiz

Identify the key terms from the clues given. *Hint*: the answers are in alphabetical order.

Key term	Definition
	This is a financial plan of expected revenue, sales or expenditure for a department or an organization, for a given period of time.
	Refers to an area or department of a business that costs can be attributed to (for reasons of accountability).
	Refers to a department or strategic business unit within an organization that functions autonomously and is held accountable for its own costs and revenues.
	Refers to discrepancies between actual outcomes and budgeted outcomes.

Task 4: Calculations and analysis

a. Complete the missing information for Vivien Jack Hair Salon.

Variable	Budgeted ($)	Actual Outcome ($)	Variance ($)	Variance (F/A)
Wages	4,000	4,200	i	Adverse
Salaries	4,500	4,500	ii	–
Stock	1,800	1,850	iii	iv
Revenue	15,750	v	290	Favourable
Direct costs	vi	2,950	250	Favourable

b. Give two examples of stock (inventory) that are likely to be held by Vivien Jack Hair Salon.

c. Give two examples of direct costs likely to be incurred by Vivien Jack Hair Salon.

Task 5: Explain …

a. The difference between budgets and forecasts.

b. Why 'positive' variances do not exist in budgeting.

c. One key advantage of zero budgeting.

d. The difference between adverse budgets and budget deficits.

e. The difference between cost centres and profit centres.

Task 6: Multiple choice

1. Which of the following best describes a budget?

- **A.** Forecast inflows and outflows of cash over the next twelve months
- **B.** The financial plan for the next twelve months
- **C.** The money available to a business for its daily operations
- **D.** The spending by the different departments of a business

2. Which statement about budgets is incorrect?

- **A.** Help managers to control operational expenses
- **B.** Help managers to plan, monitor and control business activities
- **C.** They are historical (backward-looking) financial plans
- **D.** They are set in line with the aims of the business organization

3. The budgeting system that requires budget holders to justify the money that they wish to spend is known as

- **A.** Budgetary constraint
- **B.** Flexible budgets
- **C.** Incremental budgets
- **D.** Zero budgeting

4. The budget cycle usually lasts for which period of time?

- **A.** 1 week
- **B.** 1 month
- **C.** 6 months
- **D.** 12 months

5. The difference between actual results and budgeted results is known as

A. Conflict

B. Deviation

C. Discrepancy

D. Variance

6. Which of the following is not a direct function of budgeting?

A. To anticipate costs and revenues

B. To assess performance related pay of managers

C. To ensure that managers plan ahead

D. To review progress on a regular basis

7. Which type of budget allows an organization to adjust to changes in the business environment?

A. Contingency budgets

B. Flexible budgets

C. Master budgets

D. Zero budgeting

8. When actual advertising costs are more than the budgeted figure, there is said to be a(n)

A. Favourable variance

B. Negative variance

C. Positive variance

D. Unfavourable variance

9. Which of the following is least likely to be a factor that affects how a budget is set?

A. Employer-employee negotiations

B. Historical benchmarking

C. The availability of finance

D. The budget holder's length of experience

10. When cash receipts are higher than expected or staffing costs are less than anticipated, the result is

A. Favourable variances

B. Higher profitability

C. Higher revenue expenditure

D. Shorter cash flow cycles

Unit 4.1 The role of marketing

Task 1: True or false?

		True/False
a.	Advertising is what gets a product sold.	T
b.	Consumer markets are the products directly aimed at individuals and households.	T
c.	Goods and services are marketed in the same way.	F
d.	Market leaders are firms with the largest market share within an industry.	T
e.	Market orientated businesses are more financially successful than product orientated firms.	F
f.	Marketing is concerned with selling goods and services to consumers.	T
g.	Marketing is the same as advertising and selling.	F?
h.	Markets can exist without physical locations.	T
i.	The use of commercial marketing methods to achieve the benefits of social change is called social marketing.	T
j.	The use of marketing strategies to meet the needs and wants of customers in a profitable way is called commercial marketing.	T

Task 2: Vocabulary quiz

Identify the key terms from the clues given. *Hint*: the answers are in alphabetical order.

Key term	Definition
Advertising	Type of marketing that focuses on meeting the demands (needs and wants) of customers in a profitable way.
	The guidelines that help businesses to act in a socially moral way by considering what is ethically right or wrong.
Market orientation	A marketing approach that places the needs and wants of customers as the key to success.
market growth	Increases in the size of a particular market or industry, usually expressed as the percentage increase in the market size over a given period of time.
Market share	A measure of a firm's market power, this is measured by calculating the firm's sales revenue as a percentage of all sales in the market.
	The business function of determining the products required to meet the needs and wants of customers, in a profitable or sustainable way.
Marketing plan	A document outlining the marketing mix of an organization in order to achieve its marketing objectives.
Product orientation	The marketing approach that does not respond well to change because the needs of customers and the market are not catered for.
Social marketing	Marketing activities that seek to influence social behaviour to benefit the target audience and society as a whole.

Task 3: Explain …

a. The meaning of marketing.

activities to get a product or service sold.

b. How businesses might calculate their market share.

Based on sales/output

c. One advantage and one disadvantage to a business that plans to launch new products in rapidly growing markets.

d. The difference between commercial marketing and social marketing, using smoking as an example.

Commercial marketing → sell cigarettes
Social marketing → promote dangers of smoking.

e. The difference between product orientation and market orientation.

Product orientation prioritizes R+D over consumers.
Market orientation prioritizes consumer wants + needs and involves extensive market research.

Task 4: Calculating market share

a. Complete the missing figures in the table below for a market valued at $150 million.

Company	Sales ($m)	Market share (%)
A	60	i
B	30	ii
C	iii	22
D	iv	18

b. Based on your answers to the above, calculate and comment on the two-firm concentration ratio.

Task 5: Multiple choice

1. Marketing is not about
   - A. Customer relations management
   - B. Meeting the needs and wants of consumers
   - C. Recruiting the best sales people
   - D. Understanding the needs and wants of customers

2. Which statement cannot be applied to the nature of marketing?
   - A. Customers are of central importance to marketing
   - B. It affects all functional aspects of a business
   - C. It is all about selling products to meet the needs of customers
   - D. Marketing is far more than advertising

3. The size of a market cannot be measured in terms of
   - A. Marketing budgets
   - B. Sales revenue
   - C. Sales volume
   - D. The number of customers

4. Which of the following is not part of the marketing mix for physical goods?
   - A. Distribution
   - B. People
   - C. Product
   - D. Promotion

5. The marketing mix for services does not necessarily include
   - A. Packaging
   - B. People
   - C. Physical evidence
   - D. Price

6. Which of the following is not part of the marketing mix for services?
   - A. People
   - B. Physical evidence
   - C. Place
   - D. Production

7. A key difference between goods and services is that services are

A. Homogeneous

B. Perishable

C. Purchased by the owner

D. Tangible

8. Market orientation is a marketing strategy that involves

A. Developing products based on an organization's production capabilities

B. Primary research to find out about customers' wants and needs

C. Producing goods that are innovative to meet the needs of the market

D. Researching consumers' needs in order to develop new products

9. Which statement does not apply to market orientated businesses?

A. Customer buying habits enable a firm to use appropriate promotional strategies

B. Pricing decisions consider what customers are prepared and able to pay

C. The products made by a market orientated businesses are what customers actually want or need

D. There is a lot of spending on research and development

10. Which feature cannot be applied to market orientated businesses?

A. Distribution networks make it convenient for customers to make purchases

B. Price is based on customers' ability and willingness to pay

C. Products are designed according to what the producer feels will sell

D. Research is conducted about people's needs and wants

11. Product orientated marketing means

A. Basing all marketing decisions on the needs of customers

B. Producing and marketing products that the firm believes will sell

C. Using a firm's assets to increase the marketing budget

D. Using a firm's strengths such as its brand image to market existing and new products

12. The physical element in the marketing of a service is known as the

A. Added value

B. Packaging

C. Physical evidence

D. Physical product

13. Market share can be described as

- **A.** The number of suppliers in a particular market
- **B.** The percentage of total sales in a market that can be attributed to a firm
- **C.** The relative size of a particular market
- **D.** The total sales, as measured by value or volume, in a market

14. An advantage of higher market share is that

- **A.** It can lead to market leadership
- **B.** It requires economies of scale to be earned
- **C.** The firm will operate more productively
- **D.** There will be less competitors in the market

15. Organizations trying to market healthier diets and eating habits are most likely to use

- **A.** Commercial marketing
- **B.** Market orientation
- **C.** Product orientation
- **D.** Social marketing

16. Which of the following is an example of a marketing objective for a clothes retailer?

- **A.** Improve operations management within the organization
- **B.** Increase the firm's market share by 5% within the next 18 months
- **C.** Increase output by 1 million units by the end of this year
- **D.** Open 5 new stores in Vietnam within the next three years

17. Lexi has decided to operate a franchised Le Café coffee shop in a busy commercial district. She chose to use premium pricing for its range of coffees and desserts. She also decided to advertise by distributing flyers and coupons in the local area.

Which elements of the marketing mix below have not been mentioned for the above situation?

- **A.** People, physical evidence and process
- **B.** Place, price and promotion
- **C.** Place, product and promotion
- **D.** Price, promotion and people

18. Marketing that takes account of the moral issues involved in business activity is known as

- **A.** Commercial marketing
- **B.** E-marketing
- **C.** Ethical marketing
- **D.** Social marketing

19. Some businesses are seen to have senior managers chauffeured in expensive cars, partly to portray an image of high quality and standards. This is an example of

- **A.** Financial motivation
- **B.** Packaging
- **C.** Physical evidence
- **D.** Process

20. The marketing objectives of non-profit organizations is least likely to include

- **A.** To gain higher market share
- **B.** To generate a financial surplus
- **C.** To improve brand recognition
- **D.** To increase sales turnover

Unit 4.2 Marketing planning

Task 1: Vocabulary quiz

Identify the key terms from the clues given. *Hint*: the answers are in alphabetical order.

Key term	Definition
	The moral aspects of a firm's marketing strategies. It can be encouraged by the use of moral codes of practice.
	A particular customer group within a market for a product which has shared characteristics and needs that are targeted by marketers.
	The systematic process of devising marketing objectives and appropriate marketing strategies to achieve these objectives.
	The approach taken by an organization in order to achieve its marketing objectives.
	Industries that buy and sell products catered for a large and broad range of target markets, e.g. fruits and vegetables, canned drinks, and printing paper.
	Industries that buy and sell highly specialised goods and/or services that cater for a small and select target market, e.g. wakeboarders and fencers.
	A form of non-price competition and product differentiation that focuses on the ways in which a product is presented to customers.
	A technique that shows how a product is perceived in relation to other products or brands that are available in the same market.
	A clearly identifiable group of customers that an organization focuses its marketing efforts on.
	An exclusive customer benefit that no other organization can claim for its product.

Task 2: True or false?

		True/False
a.	A marketing plan is a document outlining a firm's marketing objectives and the marketing strategies to be used to achieve these objectives.	
b.	A perception map is a graphical illustration of customer perception of a business, its products or brands in comparison to rivals in the same industry.	
c.	A product is a physical good sold by a business.	
d.	In marketing, 'place' is used to describe the methods of distributing products to customers, e.g. wholesalers, retailers and vending machines.	
e.	Marketing plans cannot work effectively without all four elements of the traditional marketing mix.	
f.	Niche markets are those that provide goods and services that appeal to an extensive number of customers.	
g.	Prices in niche markets tend to be relatively low due to the amount of competition that exists.	
h.	Psychographic segmentation splits the market according to people's lifestyle choices and personal values.	
i.	Striving for increased market share would be an example of a marketing objective.	
j.	The amount that customers pay for a particular good or service is called the cost.	

Task 3: Explain the difference between …

a. The marketing of goods and the marketing of services.

b. Marketing objectives and marketing strategies.

c. Market segments and market segmentation.

d. Targeting and market segmentation.

e. Niche marketing and mass marketing.

Task 4: Multiple choice – Market segmentation, consumer profiles and market mapping

1. Which of the following is unlikely to feature in a marketing plan?

   A. Marketing budgets

   B. Marketing goals

   C. Product extension strategies

   D. SWOT analysis

2. Elements of the traditional marketing mix do not include

   A. Distribution

   B. Process

   C. Product

   D. Promotion

3. Which of the following is not a marketing objective?

   A. Market leadership

   B. Market positioning

   C. Market segmentation

   D. Market standing

4. The marketing of services does not directly include

   A. Packaging

   B. People

   C. Physical evidence

   D. Processes

5. What is the collective name given to the various methods used by a business to distinguish itself and its products from rivals in the industry?

   A. Cost leadership

   B. Differentiation

   C. Diversification

   D. Focus

6. The collective name for all groups of customers who have the same needs and wants for a particular product is known as a

   A. Focus group
   B. Market
   C. Market segment
   D. Target group

7. The study of human population dynamics is known as

   A. Demography
   B. Geography
   C. Marketing
   D. Psychology

8. Demographic segmentation can be done in all the following ways except

   A. Age
   B. Gender
   C. Lifestyle
   D. Religion

9. Which statement below cannot be applied to market segmentation?

   A. Demographics is the most common method of segmentation
   B. It is used for primary research only
   C. Segmentation acknowledges the fact that customers are different
   D. Segmentation allows a firm to fine-tune its marketing mix

10. If a firm uses a segmentation strategy based on characteristics such as religion, gender and marital status, then it is using which type of segmentation?

   A. Demographic
   B. Ethnicity
   C. Geographic
   D. Psychographic

11. Segmentation can bring about potential advantages, except

   A. Ability to identify suitable advertising media
   B. Ability to spread risks
   C. Less waste due to focused marketing
   D. The time involved in compiling customer profiles

12. Segmentation can be split into three broad categories. Which option below is not one of the methods?

A. Academics

B. Demographics

C. Geographic

D. Psychographics

13. The image or perception of a product or brand in relation to other products or brands in the market is known as

A. Branding

B. Physical evidence

C. Positioning

D. Segmentation

14. The strategy that involves changing the perception of a product or brand relative to those offered by rival firms is known as

A. Market mapping

B. Perception mapping

C. Positioning

D. Repositioning

15. A product's location on a position map is determined by

A. Competitors

B. Consumers

C. Producers

D. Suppliers

16. If Audi is perceived as being inferior to rivals BMW and Mercedes, then the firm needs to review its

A. Corporate image

B. Demographics

C. Positioning

D. Segmentation

17. A 'premium brand' is perceived as one that offers

A. High quality at a high price

B. High quality at a low price

C. Low quality at a high price

D. Low quality at a low price

18. A 'cowboy brand' is perceived as one that offers

A. High quality at a high price

B. High quality at a low price

C. Low quality at a high price

D. Low quality at a low price

19. McDonald's introduced salads to its menu to target the more health-aware customer. This is an example of which type of segmentation?

A. Demographic

B. Geographic

C. Psychographic

D. Socio-economic

20. Which concept refers to any distinctive aspect or feature of a product that differentiates it from others that are available on the market?

A. Branding

B. Competitive rivalry

C. Monopoly power

D. Unique selling point

HIGHER LEVEL

Unit 4.3 Sales forecasting *[HL Only]*

Task 1: Vocabulary quiz

Identify the key terms from the clues given. *Hint*: the answers are in alphabetical order.

Key term	Definition
	The arithmetic mean of three consecutive numbers, such as sales revenue figures for the past three months.
	The recurring fluctuations in sales revenues due to the trade cycle (or business cycle).
	Forecasting technique used to identify the trend from past data and then extending this to predict future sales.
	The most common form of expressing an average, by calculating the sum of all numbers in the data set divided by the number of items in the data set.
	Mathematical method used to find underlying trends by smoothing out variations in a data set caused by seasonal, cyclical and random variations.
	These are unpredictable fluctuations in sales revenues, caused by erratic and irregular factors that cannot be practically anticipated.
	A quantitative management technique used to forecast a firm's level of sales over a given time period.
	These are predictable and periodic fluctuations in sales revenues over a specified time period, such as certain months or times of the year.
	A statistical technique that identifies trends in historical data, often adjusted for seasonal and cyclical fluctuations.

Task 2: True or false?

		True/False
a.	As a quantitative decision-making tool, the culture of an organization or the sub-culture of the sales department has no impact on sales forecasting.	
b.	Correlation shows the degree to which two sets of numbers or variables are related, e.g. sales revenue during different times of the year.	
c.	External influences, such as an economic recession, can cause large discrepancies and inaccuracies in sales forecasts.	
d.	Marketers can use sales forecasts to make decisions about expanding to overseas markets.	
e.	Sales forecasting is a statistical technique used to predict the level of sales over a certain time period.	
f.	Seasonal variation is a forecasting technique that identifies the trend by using past data and extending this trend to predict future sales. This is extrapolation	
g.	The 4-point moving average is $123.0 for the following data set: $121, $123, $122 and $124. $122.5	
h.	The mean is the most common measure of an average, by dividing the sum of all the numbers in a data set by the number of items in that data set.	
i.	The range is the numerical difference between the highest and the lowest values in a data set.	

Task 3: Multiple choice

1. Sales forecasting is a

   A. Decision-making tool used to calculate sales data

   B. Management tool used to extrapolate trends in certain variables

   C. Qualitative management decision-making tool

   D. Statistical tool used to predict a firm's sales level

2. Which of the following is not an example of time series data?

   A. Budgetary variations

   B. Cyclical fluctuations

   C. Random variations

   D. Seasonal variations

3. Benefits of sales forecasting do not include the direct ability to

   A. Improve productive efficiency

   B. Improve stock control

   C. Improve the management of a firm's cash flows

   D. Increase market share

4. The number that occurs more frequently than any other value in the data set is called the

   A. Mean

   B. Median

   C. Modal

   D. Range

5. Time series data is not feasible during which stage of a product's life cycle?

   A. Decline

   B. Growth

   C. Launch

   D. Maturity

6. Which of the following products is least likely to face seasonal fluctuations in demand?

   A. Banking services

   B. IB examiners and moderators

   C. School bus services

   D. Umbrellas and raincoats

HIGHER LEVEL

7. Which of the following statements is not a limitation of sales forecasting?

   A. Forecasts are rarely perfect

   B. Forecasts become less accurate the longer the time period under consideration

   C. The data make it difficult to extrapolate sales trends

   D. They are more accurate for predicting sales of single items rather than for a group of items

8. If a firm's quarterly sales revenues are $1,179, $1,281 and $2,202, then what is its three-part moving average?

   A. $1,023

   B. $1,230

   C. $1,554

   D. $2,100

9. Which of the following is not a form of qualitative sales forecasting?

   A. Consumer panels

   B. Consumer surveys

   C. Focus groups

   D. Moving averages

10. The fundamental difference between seasonal variations and cyclical variations is

   A. The assumptions behind the variations in sales revenues

   B. The duration of the repeating pattern of variations in sales revenues

   C. The magnitude of the variations in sales revenues

   D. The time of year that the variations in sales revenues occur

Unit 4.4 Market research

Task 1: Vocabulary quiz

Identify the key terms from the clues given. *Hint*: the answers are in alphabetical order.

Key term	Definition
	Type of secondary market research, namely publications that contain the latest educational research and scholarly theory.
	Type of sampling method that involves identifying the population by geographical areas.
	Marketing activities designed to discover the beliefs, perception, feelings and opinions of potential and existing customers.
	Occurs when an inappropriate sampling methodology is used, namely mistakes that are not attributed to human errors in market research design.
	The term used to describe the total number of people in a market.
	Also known as field research or bespoke research, this is market research that involves gathering new data, first-hand for a specific purpose.
	The most common form of primary research that uses a series of questions in order to collect data from a representative sample.
	The practice of selecting a small group or segment of the population for a particular market for research purposes.
	Also known as desk research, this involves the collection of second-hand data and information that already exists, gathered by others.

Task 2: True or false?

		True/False
a.	Bar charts are useful for presenting frequencies and for ease of comparison.	
b.	Desk research involves collecting new data that is in a useable format for a firm.	
c.	Field research tends to be cheaper to collect and collate than desk research.	
d.	If a firm follows an ethical code of conduct, then the collection, processing and management of data needs to done in a principled manner.	
e.	Market research can reduce risks in business decision-making because it provides better information to managers.	
f.	Organizational culture has no direct impact on market research.	
g.	Pie charts are used for expressing percentages, such as data on market share.	
h.	Questionnaires can be used to collect qualitative and quantitative data.	
i.	Sampling is used to conduct primary research. It is used because asking every person in a population to respond would be too time consuming and costly.	
j.	Skilled interviewers are required to conduct qualitative research which can be expensive as they have to be paid for their time and expertise.	

Task 3: Sampling

Identify the sampling method from the given clues...

Description	Sampling method
Dividing the population into geographical areas and taking certain regions as the sample .	
Uses subjects that are easy (simple) to reach, e.g. students often use their classmates and friends in a research study.	
Sampling a given number of people who share similar characteristics, e.g. teenagers, parents, smokers or students.	
Method that allows everyone an equal chance of being selected for sampling.	
Research carried out with individuals who then suggest other friends, family members or colleagues to increase the sample size.	
An appropriate sample, based on different market segments, is chosen to represent the views of the population.	

Task 4: Explain the difference between ...

a. Qualitative and quantitative market research.

b. Ad-hoc market research and continuous market research.

c. Quota sampling and random sampling.

d. Academic journals and market analyses.

Task 5: Multiple choice

1. What is the name given to the process of gathering, recording and analysing of data related to a good or service in order to make more informed marketing decisions?

   A. Market development

   B. Market research

   C. Marketing planning

   D. Segmentation

2. Which of the following is not a potential problem associated with primary research data?

   A. Costs

   B. Focus

   C. Researcher bias

   D. Sample size

3. Primary data is ________ research that collects ___________ data for a specific purpose.

   A. Desk, existing

   B. Desk, new

   C. Field, existing

   D. Field, new

4. Primary research is

   A. Collecting new data for a specific purpose

   B. Data that has not been processed by a firm

   C. Using experiments and observations to find out about what customers want or need

   D. Using questionnaires to collect quantitative data

5. Why might a business carry out primary research?

   A. To discover their customers' needs and wants

   B. To gain more market share

   C. To gather data required that does not already exist

   D. To produce better goods or services for their customers

6. Which of the following is an example of primary research?

   A. Customer suggestions and feedback

   B. Economic forecasts for the next twelve months

   C. Information from media articles

   D. Newly published government reports

7. Primary data has an advantage over secondary data because

   A. It is normally less time consuming to gather

   B. It is unique to the purpose of the research

   C. It saves time on data analysis

   D. The data already exists so is cheaper to gather

8. Primary data can be gathered from the use of

   A. Academic journals

   B. Government statistics

   C. Group interviews

   D. Internet websites

9. Primary data can be best gathered by

   A. Government publications

   B. Observations and surveillance

   C. Quantitative research

   D. Trade research and development

10. Which of the following is unlikely to be a drawback of primary research?

   A. Findings come from unrepresentative samples

   B. Inappropriate questions may be asked

   C. Primary research may lack specific focus

   D. Respondents may exaggerate their views

11. Primary research can be obtained by several methods except for

   A. Academic publications

   B. Focus groups

   C. Observations

   D. Photographic evidence

12. Secondary data can be gathered from the use of

   A. Focus groups

   B. Observations

   C. Social trends

   D. Suggestion boxes

13. Desk research can be conducted by

A. Accessing company annual accounts

B. Personal interviews

C. Surveys mailed through the post

D. Telephone interviews

14. Which statement below cannot be applied to desk research?

A. Data are often provided by specialist market research firms

B. Includes the latest findings from industry surveys

C. Includes the use of survey and interview findings conducted by the firm

D. Uses existing data and information for market research purposes

15. Existing market research data collected from third-party sources is known as

A. Desk research

B. Field research

C. Primary research

D. Quantitative research

16. Which of the following is not a source of secondary data?

A. Company annual reports

B. Government publications

C. Observations

D. Reference books

17. The difference between quantitative and qualitative market research is that

A. Only the former method can be statistically analysed

B. The former method uses a large sample size

C. The former relies on primary research whilst the latter relies on secondary research

D. The latter method relies on a much larger number of respondents to get a statistically valid set of answers

18. Market research that gathers the opinions, ideas, views and thoughts of consumers in a non-statistical manner is known as

A. Desk research

B. Field research

C. Qualitative research

D. Quantitative research

19. Research carried out via in-depth interviews in order to determine the reasons behind consumers' attitudes and opinions is best described as

A. Market research

B. Qualitative research

C. Quantitative research

D. Secondary research

20. Market research that gathers statistical data is known as

A. Desk research

B. Field research

C. Qualitative research

D. Quantitative research

21. The main purpose of a researcher using qualitative market research is to

A. Communicate statistical analysis of factual findings

B. Formulate organizational decision-making

C. Gather the views of a small group of people before the mass launch of a product

D. Understand the behaviour, attitudes and perceptions of selected sample

22. Which of the following cannot be applied to quantitative market research?

A. Deals with questions such as 'how much?', 'how many?' and 'how often?'

B. Is based on numerical data and information

C. Is based on only using primary research techniques

D. Uses hard data and facts to aid statistical analyses

23. What is the term given to a representative group of the population being used for market research?

A. Demographic group

B. Market

C. Sample

D. Segment

24. Sampling is used in market research because

A. A sample can be used to increase the confidence level of statistical findings

B. A sample's views are used to represent the population's views

C. It can be easier to identify trends from the sample findings

D. It is cheaper and quicker to use a sample than to survey the whole market

25. The sampling method used to interview a given number of respondents with given characteristics, such as their age and gender, is known as

A. Cluster

B. Quota

C. Random

D. Stratified

26. Which method gives each member of the public an equal chance of being selected as part of a sample?

A. Cluster

B. Quota

C. Random

D. Stratified

27. Which method is used when a population is widely dispersed across geographical locations?

A. Cluster

B. Quota

C. Random

D. Stratified

28. Which of the following is not a feature of quota sampling?

A. Choosing a specific number of people in a market segment

B. It is relatively cheap to select the sample

C. Likely to be very representative of the population

D. Samples are collected on a non-random basis

29. Stratified sampling is least likely take account of

A. Heterogeneous characteristics of a population

B. Homogenous characteristics of the population

C. Occupations

D. Race or ethnicity

30. Snowballing is

A. Primary research that builds on the work conducted by secondary researchers

B. Secondary research that mounts very quickly due to the vast amount of information that is readily available

C. Secondary research that stems from the work of primary researchers

D. Surveys or interviews carried out with individuals, who then suggest other friends, family or acquaintances to increase the sample size

31. Which of the following is not a source of sampling error?

- **A.** A small sample size being selected
- **B.** Dishonesty of respondents
- **C.** Errors made in recording data
- **D.** Researcher bias

32. Sampling errors are likely to occur if

- **A.** A representative sample is selected
- **B.** Random sampling is used
- **C.** The sample size is significantly large
- **D.** There are sampling discrepancies

33. The sampling method that relies on word of mouth to get relevant subjects (people) for a sample is known as

- **A.** Quota sampling
- **B.** Random sampling
- **C.** Snowballing
- **D.** Stratified sampling

34. The sampling methods that involves interviewing people according to a common characteristic or attribute from a specific subgroup of a population is known as

- **A.** Quota sampling
- **B.** Random sampling
- **C.** Snowballing
- **D.** Stratified sampling

35. The sampling method that allows each entity in a population to have an equal chance of being in the sample is known as

- **A.** Quota sampling
- **B.** Random sampling
- **C.** Snowballing
- **D.** Stratified sampling

Unit 4.5 The 4 Ps

PRODUCT

Task 1: Vocabulary quiz – Product

Identify the key terms from the clues given. *Hint*: the answers are in alphabetical order.

Key term	Definition
	A marketing tool for analysing the product portfolio of a business by looking at a product's market share and whether there is high or low market growth.
	The degree of customer knowledge and recognition of a particular brand in order to gain more customers.
	The strategy of using a well-established trademark (or brand) to develop and sell new products.
	This occurs when customers buy their preferred brand of a particular product and they are reluctant to switch to another brand.
	The largest cash earners for a business in the BCG Matrix, these products have high market share in low growth (mature) markets.
	Long-lasting products purchased by individuals for personal use, e.g. cars, furniture, games consoles and washing machines.
	These methods are used to lengthen the product life-cycle of a particular good or service.
	A unique graphical representation (such as a symbol, font or picture) of a business or its brand.
	The stage in the product life cycle when sales are at, or near, their maximum and there is little scope for any growth.
	A marketing strategy that tries to give a product a unique or distinctive element so that it stands out from other products in the market.
	Marketing theory that depicts the phases a typical product goes through during its commercial existence, from launch to withdrawal.

Task 2: True or false?

		True/False
a.	Brand leaders are the most popular brands in the view of the general public.	
b.	Brands are more likely to succeed than fail.	
c.	Dogs are products in the BCG Matrix that operate in low growth markets but have low market share.	
d.	M&M's chocolates are made by Mars. M&M's is therefore a brand label of the Mars company.	
e.	Most of the new products launched by well-known multinational companies are commercially successful.	
f.	Packaging can be a major form of product differentiation.	
g.	Rapid changes in technology and fashion (trends) have shortened the life cycles of products in certain industries.	
h.	The marketing strategy focused on communicating the value of a brand and what the brand stands for is called brand development.	
i.	The term 'products' can refer to both physical goods and intangible services.	

Task 3: The Boston Consultancy Group matrix

a. The Boston matrix could be useful for a business trying to manage a diverse range of products in its portfolio. True or false?

b. Products that have low market share in a high growth market are known as question marks. True or false?

c. Assuming that stars maintain their relative market share they will eventually become cash cows. True or false?

d. Product portfolio management is the responsibility of all managers in an organization. True or false?

e. According to the Boston Consultancy Group, a firm that has too many dogs will suffer from poor cash flow. True or false?

f. What is the name given to the category of products that has high or rising market share within a growing market?

____

g. Portfolio management is not used to achieve which of the following goals?

i. Maximising the profitability of the product portfolio

ii. Supporting the overall corporate strategy

iii. To determine customer perceptions of the product portfolio

iv. To provide balance in a firm's product portfolio

h. Products that have suffered from relatively inferior marketing or product quality are known as

i. Dogs

ii. Cash cows

iii. Stars

iv. Wild cards

i. Products that have high market share in a low growth market are known as

i. Cash cows

ii. Dogs

iii. Problem children

iv. Stars

j. Match the product category with its stage in the product life cycle:

A	Cash cows	i	Maturity
B	Dogs	ii	Decline
C	Stars	iii	Growth
D	Question marks	iv	Launch

Task 4: Multiple choice – Product

1. Products that are sold from one business to another in order to further the production process are known as

A. Capital goods

B. Consumer goods

C. Durable goods

D. Perishable goods

2. Non-durable products, such as fresh ice cream, are also known as

A. Consumer products

B. Convenience products

C. Perishables

D. Speciality goods

3. Which feature does not necessarily apply to fast-moving consumer goods (FMCGs)?

A. Products that are not durable

B. Products that have low profit margins

C. Products that rely on customer repurchases

D. Products that sell in high volumes

4. Convenience products that are sold in retail outlets on a daily basis are known as

A. Capital goods

B. Consumer goods

C. Fast moving consumer goods

D. Perishable goods

5. Products that require little thought, effort and expense are known as

A. Consumer goods

B. Convenience goods

C. Durable goods

D. Perishable goods

6. Speciality goods include all the following, except

A. Designer jewellery

B. Exclusive sports cars

C. Gourmet food

D. IB Science textbooks

7. Which of the following is a perishable consumer product?

A. Fresh food

B. Fridge freezer

C. Lego toys

D. Motor vehicle

8. White goods (a type of consumer durable product) do not include

A. Cookers

B. Games consoles

C. Microwaves

D. Washing machines

9. The marketing strategy used to give a product a unique or distinctive aspect so that customers can distinguish it from those offered by competitors is known as

A. Brand awareness

B. Product differentiation

C. Product orientation

D. Unique selling point

10. Pre-launch activities in the product life cycle do not include

A. Generating new ideas

B. Market research

C. Perception mapping

D. Test marketing

11. Which of the following activities does not take place during the research and development stage of the product life cycle?

A. Market research

B. Monitoring of competitors

C. Publicity

D. Test marketing

12. The stage in a product's life cycle that requires significant investment yet often incurs losses is known as

    A. Decline
    B. Growth
    C. Launch
    D. Maturity

13. Features of the launch stage for most products do not include

    A. Extensive promotion and advertising
    B. Low sales volume
    C. Market research and development
    D. Negative cash flow

14. Which of the following is a possible reason for an increase in the sales revenue of a product?

    A. Better alternatives become available on the market
    B. Fewer channels of distribution
    C. Redesigned packaging to increase the emotional value of the product
    D. Reduced prices for products with few substitutes

15. Possible strategies to reverse a decline in the sales of a product do not include

    A. Additional features added to the product, such as special or limited editions
    B. Expanding into new markets overseas
    C. Increased use of promotional strategies
    D. Increasing prices to improve the image (perception) of the product

16. The technique of using an existing brand name to launch a new or modified product is known as

    A. Brand extension
    B. Branding
    C. Product differentiation
    D. Repositioning

17. Which of the following is not an extension strategy?

    A. Advertising used to remind and entice customers to make a purchase
    B. Exporting products to overseas markets
    C. Producing new products to sell abroad
    D. Reducing prices to attract more customers

18. Decline is

A. A fall in the value of output in the economy

B. The decline in a firm's sales revenue

C. The last stage of a product's life cycle, when sales revenues fall

D. When sales revenue falls faster than the costs of production

19. A brand cannot be represented by which of the following?

A. A logo

B. A product

C. A symbol

D. Packaging

20. Which of the following is not part of new product development?

A. Market research

B. Product extension strategies

C. Research and development

D. Test marketing

21. The objectives of new product development is least likely to include

A. To gain a competitive edge

B. To increase market share

C. To increase sales turnover

D. To raise brand awareness

22. Which statement does not refer to the importance of branding?

A. It allows firms to charge above-average prices

B. It allows firms to charge lower prices to attract more sales

C. It encourages repeat purchases and customer loyalty

D. It generates a unique character or association for a product

23. What is the name given to a product that has the largest market share in a particular market?

A. Brand awareness

B. Brand leader

C. Brand loyalty

D. Global brand

24. When customers are reluctant to switch away from purchasing their favourite brand of a particular product, this is known as

A. Brand awareness

B. Brand development\

C. Brand leadership

D. Brand loyalty

25. Brands such as Gucci, Tiffany & Co., Rolex and Rolls Royce are perceived as being high in quality and high in price. These brands are known as

A. Brand extensions

B. Cowboy brands

C. Economy brands

D. Premium brands

PRICE

Task 5: Vocabulary quiz – Pricing strategies

Identify the key terms from the clues given. *Hint*: the answers are in alphabetical order.

Key term	Definition
	Setting prices to make them seem (at least slightly) lower, such as $9.95 rather than $10.00.
	Setting a high price initially and only gradually reducing prices as competitors enter the market.
	Pricing strategy used by firms with the largest market share in an industry, with other smaller firms following the price set by the market leaders.
	Charging different prices to different market segments for essentially the same product, such as peak and off-peak transportation or child and adult fares.
	Charging a very low price, perhaps below costs, to harm the sales of competitors.
	Pricing strategy that involves setting a very low price in order to gain access into a market.
	Term that describes the difference between the selling price of a product and its cost per unit.
	Setting the price of a product below its costs of production to entice customers to buy other products with high profit margins.
	Adding a fixed amount or percentage to costs of production to determine the selling price.

Task 6: True or false?

		True/False
a.	All firms can use price discrimination as a pricing strategy.	
b.	Any particular pricing strategy can only be successful if it is supported by other elements of the marketing mix.	
c.	In theory, if consumers can buy direct from the manufacturer then the price of the product would be lower.	
d.	Predatory pricing involves temporarily setting prices so low that rival firms cannot compete in a profitable way.	
e.	Price skimming is often used by businesses entering new markets.	
f.	Price skimming tends to be used for fast moving consumer goods (FMCGs).	
g.	Psychological pricing can work for almost any product, such as groceries sold in a supermarket, motor vehicles and residential property.	
h.	The percentage or a specified amount added to the costs of production is called the profit margin.	
i.	The price decision will influence the customer's perception of a product's quality.	
j.	Whichever pricing strategy is used, a business must cover its costs of production in the long run.	

Task 7: Multiple choice – Price

1. The mark-up on a product is also known as

A. Average sales revenue

B. Cost-plus pricing

C. Loss leader pricing

D. Profit margin

Questions 2–4 relate to the information given in the table.

Cost of raw materials for A2 Bakery in June

Flour	$10,600
Whipped cream	$12,000
Fresh fruits	$25,000
Output	11,900 units

2. Given the limited information, what is the break-even price?

A. $3

B. $4

C. $5

D. $6

3. Which of the following prices is not an example of cost-plus pricing for A2 Bakery?

A. $3.95

B. $4.00

C. $4.50

D. $4.95

4. If the price is set at $6 per unit, then A2 Bakery's mark-up per unit would be

A. $4

B. $6

C. 50%

D. 100%

5. Which statement cannot be applied to penetration pricing?

A. A relatively low price is set

B. It can be used to establish higher market share

C. It can be used when there are existing competitors in the market

D. Prices are set according to the average price level

6. Which short-term pricing strategy can be used by a firm that is potentially threatened by the entry of a new supplier?

 A. Penetration pricing

 B. Predatory pricing

 C. Price discrimination

 D. Price skimming

7. One purpose of using price skimming is to

 A. Enter a new market

 B. Maximise long term sales revenue

 C. Maximise short term profit margins

 D. Prevent rivals from entering the market

8. When might a business be most likely to use price skimming?

 A. To eliminate smaller rivals from the market

 B. To establish greater market share

 C. To introduce an original and unique product

 D. When it is the market leader in the industry

9. The pricing strategy that involves a firm setting prices so low that smaller competitors are forced out of the market is known as

 A. Loss leader

 B. Penetration pricing

 C. Predatory pricing

 D. Price leadership

10. Supermarkets and other retailers often sell their own branded products at a price below their costs in order to entice sales of other more profitable products. This strategy is known as

 A. Cost-plus pricing

 B. Loss leader pricing

 C. Price leadership

 D. Price skimming

11. When the same product, usually a service, is sold in different markets at different prices, this is known as

 A. Penetration pricing

 B. Price discrimination

 C. Price leadership

 D. Price skimming

12. What pricing strategy occurs when a firm charges different prices to different groups of customers for essentially the same product?

A. Mark-up pricing

B. Penetration pricing

C. Price discrimination

D. Price leadership

13. Which of the following prices is the best example of psychological pricing?

A. $0.25

B. $1.00

C. $8.50

D. $9.95

14. Which of the following is psychological pricing most likely to be suitable for?

A. Airline operators

B. Bus operators

C. Foreign exchange dealers

D. Taxi drivers

15. Price wars are associated with which pricing strategy?

A. Penetration pricing

B. Predatory pricing

C. Price discrimination

D. Psychological pricing

PROMOTION

Task 8: Complete the missing words

Promotion is about communicating marketing messages, such as adverts, with the intention of selling the ______________ of a business. There are various ______________ that can be used for this purpose, e.g. television, radio, newspapers, magazines and the ______________ (for social media and social networking). Promotion is important to ensure that a product has a high chance of succeeding in the marketplace. However, the spending has to be ______-effective because promotion can be very expensive. The objectives of promotion are to ___________ and to __________ customers about a firm's products, and to _____________ them to purchase the products.

Promotion is often categorised as _______-_____-______ (ATL) or _______-_____-______ (BTL). ATL promotion refers to paid-for promotion, e.g. commission being paid to an advertising ______________ for creating a television advertising campaign. All other forms of promotion are known as BTL promotion. Unlike ATL promotion, the firm has direct control over BTL promotional activities such as: direct mail, exhibitions, _______ __ ______ (POS) displays and sales promotions.

The _______________ _________ refers to the different aspects of an individual promotional campaign. This can include ______________ , direct marketing, personal selling and sales promotion techniques.

Task 9: Above- or below-the-line promotion?

Place a tick (✓) in the relevant column to identify whether each of the listed promotional techniques are above-the-line (ATL) or below-the-line (BTL).

Promotional technique	ATL	BTL
Billboard posters		
Branding		
Cinema		
Direct mail		
Free samples		
Guerrilla marketing		
Internet, e.g. Google and Yahoo!		
Magazines		
Merchandising		
Newspapers		
Packaging		
Personal selling		
Point of sale displays		
Public relations		
Radio		
Sales promotion		
Social media, e.g. Twitter and Facebook		
Sponsorship		
Television		
Trade journals		
Viral marketing		
Website (company-owned)		

Task 10: Short-answer questions

a. Explain the importance of promotion in the marketing mix.

b. Distinguish between persuasive and informative advertising.

c. Explain why top sports clubs, such as Real Madrid Football Club or New York Yankees, would not want or accept sponsorship deals with a tobacco firm.

d. Suggest to a sole trader why the use of television advertising is unlikely to be a feasible promotional technique.

e. Outline two reasons why BOGOF (buy one get one free) deals are not feasible for most businesses or products.

f. Explain the benefit of customer loyalty schemes to both the customer and the business.

g. Despite their global dominance, why do well-established market leaders such as Coca Cola, Nike and McDonald's, continue to advertise?

____

____

____

____

Task 11: True or false?

		True/False
a.	Advertising clutter is a drawback of using magazines as a form of above the line promotion.	
b.	Advertising is another word for promotion.	
c.	Below the line promotion includes: direct mail, point of sales displays and flyers (handouts).	
d.	Direct marketing does not include media advertising.	
e.	Guerrilla marketing is any form of free promotion.	
f.	National television advertising is usually too expensive as a form of promotion for most businesses to use.	
g.	Packaging is often used as a form of below the line promotion.	
h.	Promotion is defined as business activities aimed at establishing and protecting the desired image of an organization.	
i.	The internet is an example of below the line promotion.	
j.	Viral marketing is usually conducted via the Internet, e.g. emails, social media and social networks.	

Task 12: Multiple choice – Promotion

1. Which of the following is not part of promotion?

A. Advertising

B. Branding

C. Price reductions

D. Public relations

2. Below-the-line promotion does not include

A. Branding

B. Cinema advertising

C. Direct mail

D. Packaging

3. Direct mail, point of sale displays and sales promotions are all examples of

   A. Above the line promotion

   B. Advertising

   C. Below the line promotion

   D. Direct marketing

4. Promotion carried out through independent media such as commercial radio is known as

   A. Above the line

   B. Advertising

   C. Below the line

   D. Broadcasting

5. Above-the-line promotion is

   A. Any form of commercial television or radio promotions

   B. Promotional techniques within the control of the organization

   C. The use of promotion via the mass media

   D. Used to persuade or inform customers of a firm's products

6. Direct marketing is

   A. Any form of above the line promotion

   B. Any form of below the line promotion

   C. Tthe marketing process of selling straight to potential and known customers

   D. Using radio, television and newspapers to sell directly to customers

7. Sales promotion can be best described as

   A. Advertising using mass media to attract customers to buy a firm's products

   B. Marketing techniques aimed directly at selling to customers

   C. Selling products at reduced sales prices to attract customers

   D. The process of persuading people to buy a firm's products

8. The catchphrase "*Have it your way*" is used by Burger King. This is an example of

   A. A corporate slogan

   B. A patent

   C. Above the line promotion

   D. Direct marketing

9. Which option best defines a business logo?

   A. A catchphrase that represents a business

   B. A registered trademark of a business

   C. A sign or symbol that represents a business and its products

   D. A verbal representation of a business

10. Telesales and telemarketing are examples of

    A. Above the line promotion

    B. Direct marketing

    C. Flexible working practices

    D. Paid-for advertising

11. Advertising strategy is least likely to consider

    A. Customer relations management

    B. Finance or budgetary constraints

    C. The costs of producing and broadcasting the campaign

    D. The types of media to be used

12. The sales method of offering a complimentary product to customers when they buy another product is known as

    A. Complementary goods

    B. Customer loyalty schemes

    C. Free gifts

    D. Sales promotion

13. Above-the-line advertising techniques do not include

    A. Celebrity or hero endorsements

    B. Personal selling techniques

    C. Sexual attraction or appeal

    D. Use of catchphrases and slogans

14. Firms such as Adidas, Pepsi, Police (sunglasses), Gillette and Marks & Spencer use celebrities to promote their products. This is an example of

    A. Hero endorsement

    B. Publicity

    C. Sales promotion

    D. Sponsorship

15. When an organization pays to be associated with a particular event or cause (such as the FIFA World Cup or the Olympic Games) in return for prominent publicity, this is known as

A. Charitable donations

B. Financial aid

C. Social marketing

D. Sponsorship

16. What is meant by public relations?

A. Activities aimed at establishing and protecting a firm's corporate image

B. Activities aimed at getting the business mentioned in the media

C. The relationship between workers and employers of an organization

D. The relationship established between customers and the business

17. Using sales material such as posters and display stands to promote a product in the place where it can be bought is an example of

A. Above the line promotion

B. In-store advertising

C. Sales promotion

D. Social marketing

18. Which of the following does not apply to informative advertising?

A. Allows customers know about a product's characteristics, purpose and functions

B. Focuses on promoting the brand or business itself, rather than a particular product

C. Tries to let customers be aware of the availability of a product

D. Used by non-profit organizations to influence people's attitudes and behaviours

19. Advertisements that attempt to get customers to purchase a product are best known as

A. Below the line

B. Informative

C. Persuasive

D. Pester power

20. The use of people to sell a firm's products directly to customers is known as

A. Direct promotion

B. Door-to-door promotion

C. Personal selling

D. Sales promotion

21. Introductory offers, such as free installation and 3 months free viewing of pay-per view television programmes, are examples of which type of promotion?

A. Above the line promotion

B. Direct marketing

C. Sales promotion

D. Television advertising

22. An advantage of using radio adverts compared with television commercials is the ability to

A. Cater for customers in diverse geographic locations

B. Engage audiences from around the world

C. Grab the attention of audiences by combining visual and audio effects

D. Reach audiences engaged in other activities, such as driving

23. The use of gaining internet traffic through social media websites such as Facebook and Twitter is called

A. Public relations

B. Social media marketing

C. Viral marketing

D. Word of mouth marketing

24. LinkedIn allows professionals and businesses to network online by sharing their professional profiles and discussion forums. Therefore, LinkedIn is an example of

A. Peer to peer marketing

B. Social marketing

C. Docial networking

D. Viral marketing

25. Which statement below does not apply to guerrilla marketing?

A. It is a form of above the line promotion

B. It is controversial as unethical methods are sometimes used

C. It is often very inexpensive or even free of charge

D. It uses untraditional (unconventional) but creative methods of promotion

PLACE

Task 13: Complete the missing words

Place, also known as ____________________, refers to the component of the marketing mix that deals with getting the right products to the customer in the most ____________________and most cost-effective way. Firms do this through different _____________, of distribution, such as the use of wholesalers, retailers and sales agents.

___________________ are people or organizations that act on behalf of sellers and buyers. _______________, for example, are the buyers of products from a manufacturer and sell on these products in smaller units to _______________. This is an example of a ______-level channel between producer, wholesaler, retailer and consumers.

____________________ refers to the use of telephone calls to clients to sell products directly to potential customers. This distribution method has proved to be popular with insurance and banking firms. The advantage of using this approach is that it ____________________ the need for sales people to make personal visits, thereby saving travel time and money.

Task 14: True or false?

		True/False
a.	A limitation of using wholesalers is that the producer takes a risk in passing on the responsibility of marketing its products.	
b.	A shorter distribution channel ensures the manufacturer has more control over the marketing of its products.	
c.	Agents are independent intermediaries who help to sell a vendor's products in return for commission.	
d.	Cost-cutting is an important element of place in the marketing mix.	
e.	Distribution is one of the four main elements of any marketing mix.	
f.	E-commerce (business via the Internet) is a form of distribution channel.	
g.	Intermediation will tend to raise the marketing costs to a business.	
h.	Manufacturers use intermediaries because they cannot sell directly to consumers.	
i.	There are only two parties involved in a two-channel chain of distribution.	
j.	Retailers are intermediaries that buy products from a manufacturer and sell these in smaller quantities to other businesses.	

Task 15: Explain ...

a. One advantage and one disadvantage to customers of using the internet to order fresh fruits and vegetables from a local supermarket.

____

____

____

____

b. The type of pricing strategy that wholesalers are most likely to use.

____

____

____

____

c. Why a long chain of distribution is not suitable for distributing perishable products.

____

____

____

____

Task 16: Vocabulary quiz – Place

Identify the key terms from the clues given. *Hint*: the answers are in alphabetical order.

Key term	Definition
	Also called brokers, these intermediaries are negotiators who help to sell a vendor's products, such as real estate agents selling commercial land.
	The means (methods) by which a product gets from the manufacturer to the consumer, such as through retail outlets or distributors.
	Also known as multiple retail stores, these retailers have numerous outlets in different locations, thus benefit from brand recognition.
	Also known as placement, this is the process of getting the right products to customers at the right time and place.
	This involves sending promotional material, such as catalogues, via the postal system to entice customers to buy a firm's products.
	Agents or firms that act as a middle person in the chain of distribution between the producer and consumers of a product.
	Specialist storage machines that stock a small range of products. These can be easily placed in almost any location.
	Direct distribution network that does not use any intermediaries, i.e. producers sell directly to their consumers.

Task 17: Multiple choice – Place

1. Traditional channels of distribution do not include

- **A.** Agents
- **B.** Distributors
- **C.** Marketers
- **D.** Wholesalers

2. Placement in the marketing mix does not refer to

   A. Distributors

   B. Retailers

   C. The location of business

   D. Wholesalers

3. Which of the following distribution channels is most suitable for luxury products such as designer clothing?

   A. One-level distribution channels

   B. Online websites

   C. Specialist retail outlets

   D. Supermarkets

4. The channel of distribution used to sell products to an end user is known as a

   A. Distributor

   B. Purchaser

   C. Retailer

   D. Wholesaler

5. Features of a wholesaler do not include

   A. Being suppliers to retailers

   B. Buying large quantities of goods and selling these in smaller quantities

   C. Charging commission for their services

   D. The ability to benefit from economies of scale

6. Which of the following is not an example of agents?

   A. Cashiers at a supermarket

   B. Financial advisors

   C. Residential real estate negotiators

   D. Travel insurance brokers

7. Consumer durables such as fridges, cookers and microwave ovens are usually distributed using

   A. Agents

   B. Direct marketing

   C. Retailers

   D. Supermarkets

8. Wholesalers buy products from manufacturers in large quantities and sell these onto retailers in smaller units. This service is known as

   A. Breaking bulk

   B. Direct selling

   C. Distribution

   D. Purchasing

9. Businesses that offer online payment methods via their internet website are using which form of placement?

   A. Direct

   B. Indirect

   C. Specialist retail

   D. Vending

10. Which of the following relates to the use of direct marketing?

    A. Customers tend to read most direct marketing mail

    B. Distribution costs are high due to the need for specialist labour

    C. High response rates

    D. Reduces the need for an intermediary

11. Which channel of distribution trades directly with household customers?

    A. Distributors

    B. Retailers

    C. Vendors

    D. Wholesalers

12. Which statement does not apply to retailers?

    A. They are an intermediary in the chain of distribution

    B. They deal directly with consumers

    C. They focus on consumer markets

    D. They rely on the expertise of distributors and agents

13. An advantage of using vending machines as a distribution method is that

    A. It is dependent on machinery working effectively

    B. Sales people are not required to sell the product

    C. The storage capacity is low

    D. they rely on the expertise of distributors and agents

14. Which distribution channel is least likely to be used by a producer of expensive products?

A. Agents

B. E-commerce

C. Retailers

D. Wholesaler

15. Wholesaling is popular in the industry for which product?

A. Garden furniture

B. Motor vehicles

C. Newspapers and magazines

D. Wedding cakes

Unit 4.6 The extended marketing mix *[HL Only]*

HIGHER LEVEL

Task 1: Explain ...

a. The difference between a service and a good.

b. The difference between the marketing of goods and the marketing of services.

c. The importance of employee-customer relationships in marketing a service.

d. Why waiting (queuing) time is an important aspect of process in the extended marketing mix.

Task 2: True or false?

		True/False
a.	'People' in the extended marketing mix refers to the employees who interact with customers, thereby delivering a service to customers.	
b.	A service is a tangible product supplied by a business, e.g. bus rides, library facilities, theatre shows, and foreign holidays.	
c.	Corporate culture and regional cultures have no direct impact on how people (employees) interact with customers.	
d.	Inadequacies in employee-customer relationships make it more difficult for the business to market its products and services.	
e.	People, processes and physical evidence are all vital in determining whether customers make repeat purchases.	
f.	Physical evidence refers to the tangible aspects of a service, such as the décor of the building.	
g.	Process in the extended marketing mix refers to the way in which a service is provided or delivered to customers.	
h.	Service-orientated businesses tend to be labour-intensive, which can be costly to the organization.	
i.	Services are heterogeneous whereas goods can be homogeneous.	
j.	The provision of good quality services relies on the goodwill of all employees.	

Task 3: Multiple choice

1. Which of the following is not a service?

   A. Assistance to seats in the cinema

   B. Purchasing popcorn and drinks at the cinema

   C. Using the washroom facilities at the cinema

   D. Watching a movie at the cinema

2. Which of the following is not a feature of a service?

   A. Durable

   B. Heterogeneous

   C. Intangible

   D. Perishable

3. The effectiveness of people in marketing or delivering a service can be measured by

   A. Customer feedback

   B. Physical eCvidence associated with the service

   C. The firm's training budget

   D. The number of employees in the firm

4. Process in the extended marketing mix is about

   A. Demonstrating the benefits of a particular service to customers

   B. Payment methods available to customers to pay for the service they receive

   C. The norms (or way things are done) within an organization

   D. The way in which a service is provided or delivered by a business

5. The degree of attentiveness, care and politeness of staff towards their customers is termed as

   A. After-sales customer care

   B. Customer relations management

   C. Delivery processes

   D. Human resource management

6. The tangible aspects of a service are known as

   A. Packaging

   B. Paraphernalia

   C. Physical evidence

   D. Processes

7. Which organization is least likely to rely on physical evidence in its marketing mix?

   A. Amazon.com

   B. Arsenal Football Club

   C. Harvard University

   D. Shangri La Hotels

8. The 'People' category in the extended marketing mix is least likely to be affected by

   A. Flexible working practices

   B. Leadership and management styles

   C. Organizational culture

   D. Training and development

9. Why do service-orientated businesses have to pay increasing attention to internet technologies?

   A. B2B provides many more opportunities for growth and evolution

   B. International marketing relies heavily on internet technologies

   C. Internet technologies help to reduce cultural differences in consumer purchasing habits

   D. Social media and social networks have empowered customers globally

10. Quality assurance is important for service-orientated businesses because

    A. Correcting mistakes is highly expensive

    B. Labour costs are very high

    C. Measuring productivity is difficult

    D. Motivating people is difficult

Unit 4.7 International marketing

Task 1: Explain ...

a. The difference between exporting and direct investment.

b. The difference between international marketing and global marketing.

c. Why fish and chips, The Royal Family, Harry Potter, James Bond and The Beatles are examples of British cultural exports.

d. Why ethics and business etiquette should be considered when a firm engages in international marketing.

Task 2: True or false?

		True/False
a.	Branding is integral to a firm's international marketing strategy.	
b.	Business etiquette refers to the mannerisms and customs by which business is conducted in different parts of the world.	
c.	Businesses need to take account of different laws and regulations when marketing overseas.	
d.	Cultural exports account for a small proportion of a country's GDP.	
e.	Franchising is a technique used by some firms to enter foreign markets.	
f.	Globalization has created many marketing opportunities for businesses.	
g.	International marketing is also known as global marketing.	
h.	Opportunities are factors in the external business environment that create prospects or openings for international marketers.	
i.	The growing presence of foreign competitors has made international marketing more important to businesses.	
j.	The mannerisms and customs (traditions) by which business is conducted in different countries is known as business ethics.	

Task 3: Odd one out

Explain which is the odd one out in each case.

a. Copyrights | Patents | Exchange rates | Health and Safety

b. Tariffs | Quotas | Embargoes | Language

c. Exporting | Joint ventures | Mergers | Takeovers

d. Exchange rates | Legislation | Unemployment | Inflation

Task 4: Multiple choice

1. Difficulties faced when exporting overseas do not include

   A. Cultural differences

   B. Fluctuating exchange rates

   C. Language barriers

   D. The sheer quantity of suitable customers

2. Which of the following is not a cultural consideration for international marketers?

   A. Business etiquette

   B. Languages

   C. Local laws

   D. Local preferences

3. Which of the following is not a socio-economic consideration for international marketers?

   A. Age distribution

   B. Attitude towards working hours

   C. Gender distribution

   D. Income levels

4. The widespread use and availability of American products overseas, such as Coca-Cola beverages or McDonald's fast food, is an example of

   A. Americanisation

   B. Cultural exports

   C. Free international trade

   D. Globalization

5. Natural barriers to international trade and exchange include

A. Business etiquette

B. Health and Safety regulations overseas

C. Import taxes

D. Trade embargoes

6. Businesses that benefit from being able to market their products in exactly the same way across the world are engaged in

A. External economies of scale

B. Global marketing

C. International marketing

D. Multilateral trade

7. The mannerisms and customs by which business is conducted in different countries and areas of the world is known as

A. Business etiquette

B. Business protocol

C. Culture

D. Internationalism

8. Which of the following is not an artificial barrier to international trade?

A. Customs duties

B. Embargoes

C. Language and culture

D. Quantitative limits

9. Opportunities of international marketing include

A. Extending a product's life cycle

B. Finding new labour

C. Large scale production

D. Marketing costs

10. Which of the following is not a cultural export?

A. American pop culture

B. Japanese just-in-time production methods

C. Mobile phones from Finland

D. Pasta and pizza meals from Italy

11. External considerations for businesses planning to market overseas do not include

- **A.** External sources of finance
- **B.** International business etiquette
- **C.** Local customs and cultures
- **D.** Trade protectionist measures

12. Which of the following methods of trade protection would not be welcomed by foreign firms if *reduced*?

- **A.** Administrative procedures
- **B.** Export restraints
- **C.** Quotas
- **D.** Tariffs

13. Tariffs are taxes on _______ goods and services and are used by governments to try to ________ their supply into a country.

- **A.** Exported, raise
- **B.** Exported, reduce
- **C.** Imported, raise
- **D.** Imported, reduce

14. Benefits to a firm in selling products internationally do not include

- **A.** Increased sales and profits
- **B.** Lower costs through international marketing
- **C.** Lower prices being charged
- **D.** Opportunities to enjoy economies of scale

15. Barriers to effective international marketing include all the following, except

- **A.** Different business laws and legislation
- **B.** Divergence in business etiquette
- **C.** Globalization of markets and cultures
- **D.** Socio and Political differences

Unit 4.8 E-commerce

Task 1: Explain …

a. How businesses can improve their productivity *and* competitiveness by using e-commerce.

b. How music retailers have been affected by e-commerce.

c. Two drawbacks of using email in the workplace.

Task 2: True or false?

		True/False
a.	B2B refers to e-commerce that takes place between businesses, rather than between businesses and consumers.	
b.	Consumer to consumer (C2C) websites earn money from charging fees to the sellers who advertise their items for sale.	
c.	Credit card payments account for the vast majority of all online purchases.	
d.	E-commerce has tended to reduce the importance of packaging in the broader marketing mix.	
e.	E-commerce is simply about trying to sell a firm's products via the Internet.	
f.	E-commerce is unsuitable for some businesses and customers.	
g.	E-commerce reduces the need for market research due to easier access to data.	
h.	High overheads can be reduced with the use of e-commerce.	
i.	Price transparency refers to the openness in communication about prices being charged by businesses.	
j.	The Internet does not necessarily provide simplicity of access for customers.	

Task 3: Multiple choice

1. Which of the products below is probably least suited to sell via the internet?

   A. Children's books

   B. DVD movies

   C. Games consoles

   D. Shoes

2. E-commerce is most suited for which type of industry?

   A. Footloose

   B. Infant

   C. Sunrise

   D. Sunset

3. E-commerce has revolutionised business processes. This concept is known as

   A. E-tailing

   B. New product development

   C. Re-engineering

   D. Value chain management

4. E-commerce has ____________ traditional channels of distribution whilst providing ____________ convenience for most customers.

   A. Lengthened, greater

   B. Lengthened, limited

   C. Shortened, greater

   D. Shortened, limited

5. A retailer that primarily uses the internet for trading is known as which type of business?

   A. B2B retailer

   B. Clicks and bricks

   C. E-tailer

   D. Vendor

6. Online trading can benefit a business in many ways. Which option below is the exception?

   A. Opportunities to increase sales revenue

   B. Price transparency for customers

   C. Providing more accurate information and updates for customers

   D. Reducing overheads such as rent and insurance

7. Inappropriate and unsolicited online publicity and internet marketing messages are known as

   A. Advertising spam

   B. Garbage in, garbage out

   C. Junk mail

   D. Pop-up adverts

8. Which option is a key disadvantage of using the Internet as an advertising medium?

   A. Advertising clutter

   B. Inability to update the advertisement

   C. The costs of online advertising

   D. The potential size of the audience

9. E-commerce is not limited by which of the options below?

   A. Connection to the internet can be slow

   B. Higher costs of overseas sales and distribution networks

   C. Inaccessibility to the internet in some locations

   D. Security concerns can discourage online trading

10. Which of the following effects of e-commerce is a potential disadvantage to businesses?

   A. Choice of promotional mix

   B. Display (promotion) of a firm's product range

   C. Price transparency

   D. Wider distribution networks

11. Benefits of the internet as a medium of marketing do not include

   A. Better control over their marketing

   B. Cheaper transportation costs

   C. Economies of scale from operating in larger markets

   D. Lower transactions costs

12. Which of the following has proved to be the smallest barrier for international e-commerce businesses?

   A. Costs of maintenance and technical staff

   B. Language

   C. Online security

   D. Set-up costs

13. Social network sites, such as Twitter and Facebook, earn most of their money from

A. B2B trading

B. B2C trading

C. Online donations

D. Selling advertising space

14. Email has revolutionised how businesses operate on a daily basis. However, it suffers from a number of disadvantages. Which option is not one of these limitations?

A. It can reduce productivity due to the amount of time used to check emails

B. It tends to discourages face to face communications

C. Spam and informal messages can clog up email inboxes

D. There are high marginal costs in sending emails

15. What is the term used to describe promotional techniques that rely on the use of online social networks, such as Facebook, Twitter and YouTube?

A. E-commerce

B. Social networking

C. Spam

D. Viral marketing

Unit 5.1 The role of operations management

Task 1: Vocabulary quiz

Identify the key terms from the clues given. *Hint*: the answers are in reverse alphabetical order!

Key term	Definition
	Takes place during the production process when the value of output to consumers is greater than the costs of production to the firm.
	Elkington's notion of three pillars of sustainability: social, ecological and economic sustainability (or people, planet and profits).
	The ability of the society to develop in such a way that it meets the social well-being needs of the current and future generations.
	The sector that provides intellectual, knowledge-based activities to generate and share information, e.g. R&D, consultancy services and scientific research.
	The function of business concerned with providing the right goods and services in the right quantities and at the right quality level in a cost-effective way.
	The ability of the economy to develop in such a way that it meets the economic well-being needs of the current and future generations
	Capacity of the natural environment to cope with meeting the needs of the current generation without jeopardising those of future generations.
	Choice of production method when a firm relies mainly on the use of machinery and equipment to produce its output, rather than labour.

Task 2: True or false?

		True/False
a.	Ecological sustainability requires efficient and sensible use of the world's scarce resources so that they do not become exhausted (overused).	
b.	Green technologies and recycling have an important role in ensuring sustainable production to meet the needs of people today and those of future generations.	
c.	Inefficient firms can be profitable, but not in a sustainable way.	
d.	Labour intensive production means firms hire more people than any other factor of production. It is the value (amount) spent that is measured.	
e.	Modern management thinking has led to business strategy to consider more efficient and sustainable production	
f.	Operations management refers to the process of organizing production resources in order to manufacture goods and/or provide services.	
g.	Social sustainability enables production to optimize the quality of life for people and their descendants.	
h.	The role of operations management impacts on all functional areas of a business.	
i.	The role of operations management is to turn factors of production into the output of goods and services in a cost-effective way.	
j.	The tertiary sector provides services, so is not considered to be part of operations management.	

Task 3: Multiple choice

1. Which stage of production does operations management apply to?

   A. All of the below

   B. Primary

   C. Secondary

   D. Tertiary

2. Operations management strategies and practices do not include

   A. Ecological sustainability

   B. Economic sustainability

   C. Social sustainability

   D. Technological sustainability

3. The manufacturing or provision of a product that relies heavily on human resources, such as teaching and legal services, is known as

   A. Capital intensive production

   B. Labour intensive production

   C. Operations management

   D. The transformation process

4. Categories of factors of production do not include

   A. Capital

   B. Entrepreneurship

   C. Innovations

   D. Labour

5. Which of the following is not an example of labour?

   A. Entrepreneurship

   B. Intellectual ideas

   C. Manual workers

   D. Skilled labourers

6. Which production concept promotes intergenerational equity?

   A. Continuous improvements

   B. Production planning

   C. Quality management

   D. Sustainability

7. Which of the following is not an example of sustainable business practices?

   A. Cradle to cradle manufacturing

   B. Cradle to grave manufacturing

   C. Green technologies

   D. Recycling, reusing and reducing

8. What is the fundamental barrier to sustainable production in the world economy?

   A. Limited sources of finance

   B. Population growth

   C. Unethical business practices

   D. Vague business objectives

9. Which concept measures how well a business uses its resources in the production process?

   A. Conservation

   B. Efficiency

   C. Production planning

   D. Sustainability

10. Which of the following is not a role of operations management?

   A. To add value in the transformation process

   B. To ensure there are quality management processes

   C. To hire the best (most suitable) production workers

   D. To investigate the most cost-effective production methods

Unit 5.2 Production methods

Task 1: Complete the missing words

There are several methods of production. _____ production involves the customization of an individual product, from start to finish, to meet the specific requirements of a customer. Clients are likely to pay relatively ______ prices for the purchase of such ______ products.

_________ production and mass production methods both benefit from _______ of scale through larger levels of _______ . However, the marketing mix will differ, as there is less uniqueness or exclusiveness. _____ production, in particular, suffers from the _________ of output and hence relatively lower prices are charged (so relatively lower _______ margins are earned).

__________ manufacturing is an adaptation of mass production whereby tasks are completed by teams (or cells) that are given the responsibility for completing a part of the overall _________ process. In reality, this method of production tends to be _________ intensive.

Task 2: True or false?

		True/False
a.	Cellular production is a technique that involves teams of people working on a certain section of the production process, but completing a whole unit of work.	
b.	Customized production suffers from the high costs of labour intensity.	
c.	Labour productivity can be improved by investing in better training, equipment and motivation in the workplace.	
d.	Large scale (mass) production typically involves customisation of products.	
e.	Lean production methods have led to an increase in the use of job production.	
f.	Manufacturing output tends to be more cost effective when using labour-intensive technologies.	
g.	Mass production is ideal for the production of homogeneous products.	
h.	Private tuition for examination preparation is an example of job production.	
i.	Production refers to the manufacture of a physical good.	
j.	With flow production, when one task is finished, the next task must start immediately.	

Task 3: Explanations

Turner & Taylor Clothing Co. design and manufacture trendy fashion clothing for teenagers in a variety of designs, colours and sizes.

a. Identify the production method that is most likely to be used by Fabrice & Taylor Clothing Co.

____

____

b. Outline two benefits of this production method to Fabrice & Taylor Clothing Co.

____

____

c. Explain why a high level of work-in-progress means Fabrice & Taylor Clothing Co. is likely to face liquidity problems.

Task 4: Multiple choice

1. Which of the following is not an advantage of job production?

   A. Each item can be uniquely designed and produced

   B. Economies of scale can be enjoyed due to the size of the project

   C. Products can be made to match customer specifications

   D. Workers may be motivated by the variety and challenge of the project

2. All of the following are involved in job production, except for

   A. Architects

   B. Bakers

   C. Painter and decorators

   D. Private tutors

3. Which of the following is not a feature of job production?

   A. Likely to be a unique, one-off product

   B. Likely to be relatively expensive

   C. Meets the specific requirements of a customer

   D. Relatively quick to produce

4. An important feature of job production is the

   A. Distinctive quality and output

   B. High and stable levels of demand

   C. High levels of output for a mass market

   D. Repetitive and monotonous tasks

5. Job production is likely to involve

   A. A high number of orders

   B. Extensive economies of scale

   C. Labour intensity

   D. Low profit margins

6. Which of the following is not necessarily a disadvantage of job production?

   A. Economies of scale are very limited if at all attainable

   B. Highly skilled (and expensive) labour is used

   C. Production is capital-intensive

   D. Production is relatively expensive and time consuming

7. Clothing companies that specialise in producing casual clothing for the general public are most likely to use which method of production?

   A. Batch

   B. Flow

   C. Job

   D. Mass

8. Which business is least likely to use batch production?

   A. Chan's Bakery

   B. Charnley's Hair Salon

   C. Ducie's Fruit Farm

   D. Sharma's Seafood Buffet

9. Mass production does not suffer from high

   A. Average costs

   B. Fixed costs

   C. Running costs

   D. Set-up costs

10. Which of the following is not associated with flow production?

    A. Capital intensity

    B. Exclusivity

    C. Production line

    D. Standardisation

11. Mass production does not benefit from

    A. Large volumes of standardised output

    B. Lower average costs of production through economies of scale

    C. Stockpiling of manufactured products

    D. Use of easily recruited and trained workers

12. Mass production does not involve

A. Large scale production

B. Standardisation of production

C. Use of a highly skilled labour force

D. Use of capital-intensive technologies

13. Cellular manufacturing is best described as

A. Production based on capital-intensive methods

B. Production based on labour-intensive methods

C. Production processes broken down into units based around teams

D. Specialisation and division of labour in the production process

14. When workers are organized into multiskilled teams in the production process, it is known as

A. Cellular production

B. Customized production

C. Flow production

D. Process production

15. Which statement does not apply to cell production?

A. A team of workers carry out their assigned tasks

B. Employees work independently to avoid distractions

C. There is responsibility for quality assurance

D. There is supervisory support and responsibility

16. All other things being equal, businesses might be more inclined to develop capital-intensive methods of production if

A. Capacity utilization falls

B. Interest rates fall

C. Labour productivity increases

D. Wage rates fall

17. Which of the following is least likely to be standardized in the production process?

A. A bridal magazine

B. Canned soft drinks

C. McDonald's Happy Meals

D. School reports

18. What are 'idle' resources?

A. Machinery and equipment that have broken down

B. Old or outdated machinery and capital equipment

C. Poor quality resources

D. Resources that are not used in a cost-effective way

19. Which of the following is most likely to be of greater concern to a business that is deciding whether to become more capital intensive?

A. Whether the financial returns from the investment justifies the expenditure

B. Whether the investment will speed up production and increase productive capacity

C. Whether the management will be able to manage the change process

D. Whether there will be increased efficiency and, therefore, less wastage

20. Which of the following industries is the most capital intensive?

A. Fashion design

B. Management consultancy

C. Steel manufacturing

D. Travel and tourism

21. Which of the listed occupations is the least labour-intensive?

A. Hairdressers

B. Painters and decorators

C. Printers and publishers

D. Teachers

22. Which of the following changes would be least likely to increase the productivity of a business?

A. Capital-intensive production techniques

B. Hiring more workers

C. Using automation to achieve technical economies of scale

D. Using greater specialisation and division of labour

23. Productivity can best be improved by

A. Investing in production technologies

B. Paying higher wages to all staff

C. Removing an overtime policy in the workplace

D. Replacing workers with capital equipment

24. Labour productivity will increase, at least temporarily, in the examples below. Which one is the exception?

A. Authorising more overtime work

B. Implementing performance-related pay

C. Staff training and development

D. Using more labour-intensive production methods

25. The division of a large task or project into smaller tasks, allowing individuals to concentrate on an area of expertise is known as

A. Cellular manufacturing

B. Customization

C. Process production

D. Specialization

HIGHER LEVEL

Unit 5.3 Lean production and quality management *[HL Only]*

Task 1: Complete the missing words

Quality ___________ (QA) requires the implementation of processes and systems to make certain that quality standards are met, thereby ensuring customer ______________. QA is used by a business to give customers greater ___________in the quality of the products that they buy from the organization. A firm that is able to meet QA standards will publicise this, usually with the use of international quality assurance trademarks, such as ISO ______.

At the heart of quality management are concepts such as ______ production (the elimination of___________) and ______-____-______ (a production system that removes the need to use buffer stocks by having stocks and components delivered as and when they are needed in the ___________ process). Quality management also involves all members of an organization striving to make small, continuous adjustments and improvements. This philosophy is known as ______, the Japanese term for 'change for the better' or '___________improvements'.

One other way used by businesses to manage quality is by comparing their practices or performance indicators with those of the best in the industry. This method is known as _____ _________ ___________________ (BPB), or simply 'benchmarking' for short. BPB is as a continuous process in organizations that make every effort to achieve ___________ assurance.

Task 2: True or false?

		True/False
a.	An objective of quality assurance is to reduce the need for huge Research & Development spending.	
b.	Andon is a lean production method that uses a visual control system to indicate the status of an aspect of the production process.	
c.	Cradle to cradle manufacturing is a sustainability model of production, based on natural processes which benefit the natural environment.	
d.	Kaizen and zero defects are central principles of any total quality culture.	
e.	Kaizen usually involves the implementation of quality circles.	
f.	Kanban is a lean production method that uses a card system with an inventory number attached to each component in the production process.	
g.	Lean production is the process of streamlining operations management to reduce all forms of waste and to achieve greater efficiency.	
h.	Poor quality means that a firm's prices are higher than the industry average.	
i.	Quality is a source of global competitiveness.	
j.	Quality means that a product is high-class and one of the best in its industry, such as Rolls Royce cars or Rolex watches.	
k.	The 'Kitemark' is a quality assurance standard recognised throughout the world.	
l.	The implementation of total quality management tends to reduce the level of employee motivation.	

Task 3: Explanations

a. Explain how each of the following cases outlines poor quality:

i. Poor customer service at the cinema

ii. A laptop that keeps breaking down

iii. Food that is overcooked in a restaurant

b. Explain which of the following is least likely to be a measure of quality.

A. Reliability

B. Staff turnover

C. Safety

D. Efficiency

c. Explain two costs to a firm that strives to achieve quality assurance.

d. Explain two advantages to a washing machine manufacturer that is accredited with international quality standards certification such as the ISO 9000.

HIGHER LEVEL

Task 4: Multiple choice

1. Which of the reasons below does not explain why quality is important to a business?

   A. Quality can provide a competitive advantage to the business

   B. Quality is essential in order to satisfy customers

   C. Quality means less stress to employees due to the reduced workload

   D. Quality raises the confidence level of customers

2. A product that serves its purpose in fulfilling a customer's need or desire is known as

   A. Continuous improvement

   B. Fit for purpose

   C. Best practise benchmarking

   D. Quality management

3. The customer's perception of product quality is ultimately measured by

   A. Build quality

   B. Corporate image

   C. Price

   D. Value for money

4. The effect of substandard quality includes

   A. Higher standards of customer services

   B. Higher wastage levels

   C. Improved customer relations

   D. Lower costs of production

5. Which benefit does not apply to lean production?

   A. Higher standards of customer services

   B. Higher wastage levels

   C. Omproved customer relations

   D. Lower costs of production

6. Which of the following is not a method of lean production?

   A. Just-in-time production

   B. Kaizen

   C. Mass production

   D. Quality circles

7. Which of the following is not a method of waste minimisation?

   A. Cradle to cradle manufacturing

   B. International quality standards

   C. Just-in-time production

   D. Total quality management

8. An essential feature of total quality management is

   A. Andon

   B. Corporate social responsibilities

   C. Low prices

   D. Zero defects

9. The use of traditional methods to inspect quality against required standards is known as

   A. Andon

   B. Benchmarking

   C. Kanban

   D. Quality control

10. Which statement does not apply to kanban as a method of lean production?

    A. Each item or component in the production process must have a kanban

    B. It is Japanese for 'visual card'

    C. It requires continuous improvement in the production process

    D. It shows workers what is to be produced, how much of that item is to be produced and by when it needs to be produced

Unit 5.4 Location

Task 1: Complete the missing words

The location decision is vitally important for a business because it has a direct and long-lasting impact on its costs, revenues and therefore its _________. Good location decisions require in-depth research and analysis of the costs and __________ of different places, taking both quantitative and _______________ factors into consideration.

In an increasingly globalized business world, reorganizing production takes place both nationally and internationally. There are three main ways to do this:

- _____________ is the use of an organization's own people and resources to accomplish a certain function or task which would otherwise have been _______________.
- _____________ involves relocating business functions and processes overseas. These functions can remain within the business (operating in overseas markets) or outsourced to an overseas organization.
- _______________ (or subcontracting) is the practice of transferring internal business activities to an external organization, in order to reduce _______________ and increase _______________.

Task 2: True or false?

		True/False
a.	Allowing foreign firms to locate in the domestic country is harmful to the economy as there will be unemployment.	
b.	Assisted areas are identified as areas in need of regeneration in order to boost employment opportunities.	
c.	E-commerce has enabled many more businesses to become footloose.	
d.	Ethics do not have a purpose when making international location decisions.	
e.	Firms may choose to locate overseas to exploit lower costs of labour.	
f.	High sunk costs can be a key reason for deterring relocation decisions.	
g.	Insourcing is the practice of transferring internal business activities to an external organization to reduce costs and increase productivity.	
h.	Offshoring is often associated with unethical practices, e.g. the exploitation of labour in low income countries or the use of child labour.	
i.	Outsourcing is the practice of transferring internal business activities to an external organization in order to reduce costs and to increase productivity.	
j.	The location decision is irreversible.	
k.	The time and cost of transportation is considered by managers to be more important than the physical distance between locations.	

Task 3: Explain two reasons why …

a. The cost of land in busy city centres is higher than that in more remote locations.

____

____

____

____

b. Grants and subsidies from the government might be available to businesses that locate in areas of low income and/or high unemployment.

____

____

____

____

c. The internet has made the location decision less cumbersome for many businesses.

____

____

____

____

Task 4: Multiple choice

1. Which of the following is least likely to affect the location decision for a business?

A. Availability and quality of land and hence its rental value

B. Financial incentives, such as tax allowances and government subsidies

C. Infrastructure, such as access to motorways, railways and ports

D. The need to be physically located near customers

2. Which of the following would not attract a business to a particular location?

A. External economies of scale

B. Internal economies of scale

C. Nearness to market

D. Nearness to raw materials

3. Which of the firms below would be classified as a weight-losing business?

A. Cottam's Bouncy Castles

B. Freeman's Beer Company

C. Morris Bakeries

D. Nixon Oil Company

4. Weight-losing businesses locate near the source of raw materials in order to

A. Benefit from economies of scale

B. Gain from easy access to customers

C. Gain from mass production

D. Reduce transportation costs

5. Access to air transportation is considered better than access to rail or water transport for the hauling of which product?

   A. Bulky products

   B. Durable products

   C. Extremely dangerous products

   D. Highly expensive products

6. Rail transportation is most suitable for the transportation of

   A. Bulky expensive products

   B. Heavy, bulky and durable items

   C. Items of great urgency to the client

   D. Perishable products

7. For businesses such as hypermarkets and wholesalers, the most important consideration when choosing a business location is

   A. Closeness to raw materials

   B. Cost of purchasing or renting land

   C. Local infrastructure

   D. Proximity to customers

8. Government incentives for location or relocation do not include

   A. Grants and subsidies to reduce costs of production

   B. Low or interest-free loans to encourage investment

   C. Taxes imposed on harmful by-products to protect the local community

   D. Training and development programmes for the local workforce

9. Which of the following is most likely to be a qualitative factor affecting the location decision?

   A. Availability of land

   A. Labour costs

   B. Nature of local infrastructure

   C. Transportation costs

10. Which of the following is not a quantitative factor affecting the location decision?

   A. Government financial assistance

   B. Management preferences

   C. The availability of highly skilled workers

   D. The cost of land

11. The international location decision is least likely to be affected by issues regarding

A. Cultures and etiquette

B. Industrial inertia

C. Language and cultural differences

D. The stability of exchange rates

12. When businesses locate near to other organizations that function in similar or complementary markets, this is known as

A. Clustering

B. External economies of scale

C. Infrastructure

D. Special enterprise zones

13. The name given to people or organizations that carry out outsourced work more cost-effectively than the business itself, without compromising quality, is

A. Contractors

B. Insourced manufacturers

C. Outsourced manufacturers

D. Subcontractors

14. A footloose business is one that

A. Benefits by relocating from place to place to benefit from access to raw materials

B. Cannot gain any cost advantage from a particular location

C. Gains by relocating from place to place to benefit from access to different markets

D. Moves from one country to another

15. The location decision for a footloose business does not depend on

A. Access to labour

B. Government grants and incentives

C. Proximity to the market

D. The costs of a give business location

Unit 5.5 Production planning *[HL Only]*

Task 1: Complete the missing words

The ________ chain (or logistics) refers to the sequence of activities from the production of a good or service to it being ________ to the consumer. A long supply chain increases the chances of things going wrong, so effective supply chain management helps to ________ costly mistakes to the business.

Production planning involves managers overseeing and controlling the level of stock in a business. Stocks can come in three forms: _____ __________, ______-____-__________ and ________ goods. The __________ _______ __________ (EOQ) is the level of stock that minimises the firm's average costs. Firms need to balance the costs of holding excessive volumes of stock (known as _____________) with the drawbacks of holding insufficient quantities of stock (known as a ________-_____).

Delays in the ______ time (the period of time taken for a ________ to process and deliver a stock order) will mean that stocks fall below the desired minimum level so the firm has to rely on its ________ stock.

______-____-______ control systems rely on the use of buffer stocks in order to meet changing levels of demand. By contrast, ______-____-______ systems have stocks delivered immediately the moment that they are required for production. This helps to improve the firm's _________ capital as money is not tied up in stocks, which might not be highly liquid.

Task 2: Explanations

a. Explain the difference between just-in-case (JIC) and just-in-time (JIT) stock control systems.

____

____

____

____

b. Explain the difference between outsourcing and offshoring.

____

____

____

____

c. Explain how it is possible to outsource production internationally yet keep the business growing domestically.

____

____

____

____

HIGHER LEVEL

d. Explain the probable effect on the organizational structure of a firm that subcontracts a significant portion of its operations.

e. Explain the difference between capacity utilization and productive capacity.

f. Suppose a firm has fixed costs of \$100 000 and a productive capacity of 50 000 units per month. Calculate the change in the average fixed costs of production if the firm operates at only 85% capacity compared to operating at full capacity.

Task 3: Interpreting JIC stock control diagrams

a. Identify the missing labels in the diagram below.

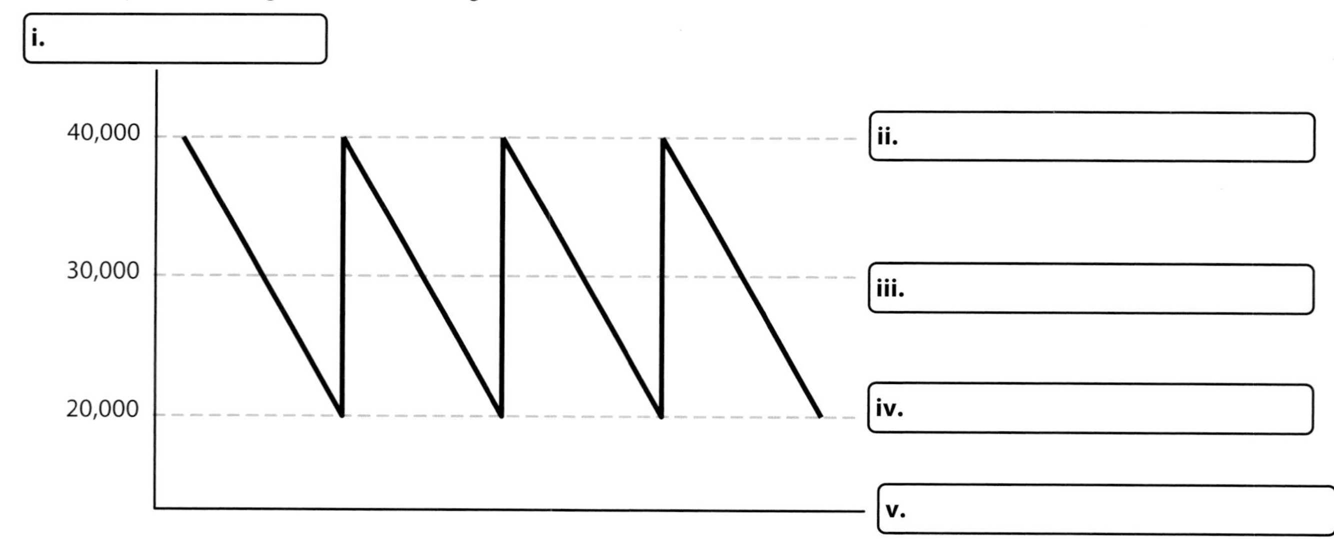

b. In the above diagram, identify the following:

i. buffer stock

ii. re-order quantity

iii. re-order level

Task 4: Multiple choice

1. Which of the following is not a type of stock for a business?

   A. Finished goods

   B. Ordinary shares

   C. Raw materials

   D. Work-in-progress

2. Drawbacks of a stock-out do not include

   A. Disgruntled customers

   B. Loss of sales

   C. Negative impact on cash flows

   D. Storage costs

3. Stockpiling means that a business

   A. Builds up excessive levels of inventory

   B. Operates at a level lower than its buffer stock

   C. Plans for a large safety margin

   D. Produces on a larger scale to benefit from cost savings

4. A drawback of holding too much stock is

   A. Inflexibility in production levels

   B. Share prices are likely to drop due to excess production

   C. Stocks are highly liquid assets

   D. Working capital is tied up in stockpiling

5. Which option is the most likely drawback of outsourcing operations to overseas firms?

   A. Major communication barrier due to geographical distances

   B. The quality of production might become more difficult to monitor

   C. They might have lower production costs

   D. They might have more skilled labourers

6. Efficiency in production is not usually measured by using which of the following measures?

   A. Labour turnover

   B. Output per machine hour

   C. Output per worker

   D. Unit costs of production

7. One advantage of using a just-in-case stock management system is that

   A. Buffer stocks can be minimised

   B. Productive efficiency is encouraged

   C. Stockpiling is less likely to occur

   D. There is flexibility to meet sudden changes in consumer demand

8. The stock handling method based on having stocks being delivered only when they are needed is known as

   A. Just-in-case

   B. Just-in-time

   C. Re-order levels

   D. Usage rate

9. Just-in-time is least likely to suffer from

   A. High administrative costs

   B. Inflexibility in meeting unexpected changes in demand

   C. Reliance on suppliers

   D. Wastage and reworking

10. The rate at which stock levels are used up in the production process is known as the

   A. Lead time

   B. Re-order level

   C. Re-order quantity

   D. Usage rate

11. The production level where unit costs are at their lowest is known as the

   A. Capacity utilization rate

   B. Economic order quantity

   C. Minimum stock level

   D. Productivity rate

12. Which incident might cause a firm to rely on its buffer stocks?

   A. Lower costs of production

   B. Shorter lead times

   C. Sudden increase in consumer demand

   D. Timely deliveries from suppliers

Questions 13–15 refer to the diagram below for Atkinson Farms Ltd:

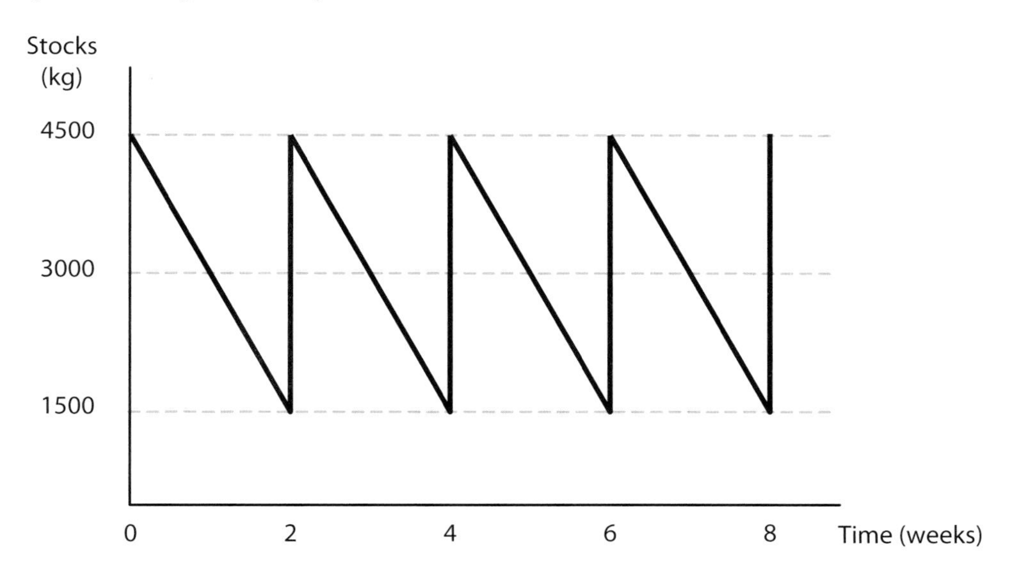

13. What is the lead time for Atkinson Farms Ltd?

A. 1 week

B. 2 weeks

C. 6 weeks

D. 8 weeks

14. What is the buffer stock for Atkinson Farms Ltd?

A. 1,500 kg

B. 3,000 kg

C. 4,500 kg

D. Zero

15. What is the re-order quantity of Atkinson Farms Ltd?

A. 1,500 kgs

B. 3,000 kgs

C. 4,500 kgs

D. zero

16. A disadvantage of low capacity utilization is

A. Higher average fixed costs of production

B. Higher fuel and energy bills

C. Higher indirect costs of production

D. Overtime payment to staff

HIGHER LEVEL

17. If a firm's maximum productive capacity is 35 000 units per month but it actually produces 28 000 units per month, then its capacity utilization is

A. 125%

B. 80%

C. 25%

D. 20%

18. Which option is most likely to be a threat for a restaurant operating at full capacity?

A. Food quality will fall

B. Queuing times will increase

C. Staffing costs will rise

D. Working capital will be limited

19. Capacity utilization for a business facing high growth rates could be improved by

A. Holding lower levels of stock

B. Reducing lead times

C. Subcontracting work

D. Using just-in-time stock control

20. Firms with _____ profit margins and _____ levels of break-even will benefit from high capacity utilization.

A. High, High

B. Low, Low

C. High, Low

D. Low, High

21. What is the term given to the practice of reassigning business operations to an external firm in order to improve cost effectiveness?

A. Delegation

B. Offshoring

C. Portfolio working

D. Subcontracting

22. Which of the following is not a reason for offshoring?

A. Consideration and observation of overseas regulations

B. Reduced production costs

C. The use of specialist labour

D. Workforce flexibility

23. Which of the following is not a quantitative method that can be used to help with decisions about the cost to make (CTM) and cost to buy (CTB)?

A. Break-even analysis

B. Cost benefit analysis

C. Investment appraisal

D. Ratio analysis

24. Subcontracting does not benefit from

A. Extra labour flexibility

B. Greater job security

C. Improved labour productivity

D. Lower unit costs of labour

25. The outsourcing of business activities to an external agency or third party that is located overseas is known as

A. Globalization

B. Offshoring

C. Outsourcing

D. Subcontracting

Unit 5.6 Research and development *[HL Only]*

Task 1: Complete the missing words

__________ is about investigating the unknown, such as new products or processes. ______________ is about using research findings to create new products that might be commercialised. The purpose of ___________ and _____________ (R&D) is to provide continual advancements in production and to launch new products to satisfy customer needs in a __________ way. ______________ is the commercialisation of these new processes, products or ideas.

In order to provide inventors with an incentive to innovate, the legal system controls and enforces the use of intellectual __________ ________ (IPRs), such as ____________ and ____________. People or firms wishing to use the IPR of others must first seek the legal permission of the IPR holder. For instance, _________ give an entrepreneur or a business the exclusive and legal right to produce a new product or to use a particular production process. Intellectual property rights are recorded on a firm's _________ ______, under the section of intangible fixed assets.

Task 2: True or false?

		True/False
a.	Adaptive creativity refers to incremental innovations, which adjust or develop a product or process that already exists.	
b.	Changing the context of a product by a repositioning strategy is known as positioning innovation.	
c.	Copyright is legal protection for written pieces of work such as literature to protect the property rights of the creator.	
d.	Expenditure on research and development leads to higher sales revenues.	
e.	Innovation usually stems from creativity.	
f.	Making modifications or improvements to existing products is known as product research.	
g.	Operating in an unfilled niche market is an example of innovative business practice.	
h.	Patents give the registered owner the exclusive right to commercialise a particular invention, for an agreed length of time.	
i.	Radical innovative change that alters the nature of specific markets is known as paradigm innovation.	
j.	Research and development expenditure is justified in sunset industries.	

Task 3: Explain ...

a. Why direct marketing is more suitable than television advertising for marketing products to early adopters of new innovations.

____

____

____

____

b. Why research and development is usually a prerequisite to the successful launch of a new product.

c. Two limitations of research and development to a firm with minimal market share.

d. Two benefits of innovation.

Task 4: Multiple choice

1. Research and development is unlikely to include which of the following?

A. Market research

B. Position mapping

C. Prototypes

D. Test marketing

2. The most likely purpose of spending huge amounts of money on research and development is to

A. Diversify the activities of a business

B. Gain rights to patents, trademarks or copyrights

C. Increase the earning potential of the business in the future

D. Remove competition

3. Research and development expenditure is often used as a barrier to entry by large businesses that dominate the market. What are these firms known as?

A. Market leaders

B. Process innovators

C. Sunrise businesses

D. Sunset businesses

HIGHER LEVEL

4. Innovation is best described as

A. Market-orientated processes

B. New products that are launched on the market

C. The commercial development and use of an idea or process that appeals to consumers

D. The development of new ideas and working practises

5. Benefits of innovation do not include

A. Brand switching

B. Growth opportunities

C. Productivity gains

D. Reduced product failure rate

6. Which of the following is the least likely long-term benefit to an innovative firm?

A. Establishing a unique selling point

B. Establishing brand loyalty

C. Growth opportunities

D. Improved competitiveness

7. Which of the following is not a constraint of innovation?

A. Budgetary constraints

B. Competitiveness

C. High failure rate

D. High R&D costs

8. Which type of innovation refers to changes in the way that production takes place, i.e. how production takes place?

A. Paradigm innovation

B. Positioning innovation

C. Process innovation

D. Product innovation

9. Drastic and extensive innovations that involve high risks to a business are known as

A. Paradigm innovation

B. Positioning innovation

C. Process innovation

D. Product innovation

10. Which of the following would not qualify to be protected by copyrights?

A. Hollywood movies

B. Medicines and vitamins

C. Photographs

D. Radio broadcasts

11. A newly invented process or product that is legally and exclusively assigned to the producer is known as a

A. Copyright

B. Patent

C. Property right

D. Trademark

12. German car manufacturer Volkswagen uses the 'VW' logo as part of its marketing. What does this represent to the company?

A. A copyright

B. A patent

C. A trademark

D. An invention

13. In which financial account do companies record their intellectual property rights?

A. Balance sheet

B. Cash flow forecast

C. Income statement

D. Profit and loss account

14. What is the name given to the category of incremental innovation that adjusts or develops something that already exists?

A. Adaptive creativity

B. Innovative creativity

C. Paradigm innovation

D. Research and development

15. What is the name given to the category of innovation that involves creating something that is new?

A. Adaptive creativity

B. Innovative creativity

C. Paradigm innovation

D. Research and development

HIGHER LEVEL

Unit 5.7 Crisis management and contingency planning *[HL Only]*

Task 1: True or false?

		True/False
a.	A properly prepared contingency plan is the first step to being prepared to manage a crisis.	
b.	Careful planning can help an organization to reduce the risks of a crisis.	
c.	Contingency planning is also known as crisis management.	
d.	Contingency planning uses up valuable management time and resources, thereby increases costs.	
e.	Crisis management is about dealing with threats and disasters facing a business.	
f.	Crisis management occurs during and after an event, such as the outbreak of a fire.	
g.	Effective communication with all key stakeholders is critical in a crisis situation, such as contacting the emergency services and insurers.	
h.	Having insurance is a possible solution to a crisis situation.	
i.	Irrespective of their size, all businesses face threats.	
j.	It is important to select an appropriate team to handle disaster recovery.	
k.	Public relations play a vital part in crisis management.	

Task 2: Case study

Mattel Inc., one of the world's biggest toy manufacturers, faced more than 28 separate product recalls during 2007, upsetting consumers and retailers alike. It was reported that a public relations team of 16 people was set up to call reporters, alongside press releases and teleconference calls. Mattel's CEO, Robert Eckert, also conducted television interviews and telephone calls with individual news reporters. By the summer of 2008, the product recall crises seemed to have been forgotten.

a. Identify three stakeholder groups from the case study.

____

____

____

b. Explain what is meant by a product recall and why is it an example of a crisis.

____

____

____

____

c. Outline two reasons why crisis management and contingency planning are important to global multinational companies such as Mattel Inc.

Task 3: Multiple choice

1. The way in which an organization responds to a crisis is known as

   A. Business planning

   B. Contingency planning

   C. Crisis management

   D. Operational management

2. The systematic attempt to prevent or to manage crises should they occur is known as

   A. Contingency planning

   B. Crisis management

   C. Damage recovery management

   D. Workforce planning

3. Which of the following is not a characteristic of a crisis to an organization?

   A. Anticipated

   B. Element of surprise

   C. Threatening

   D. Unpredictable

4. A crisis is least likely to occur in which of the following cases?

   A. Conflict with key contractors

   B. Industrial espionage

   C. Public relations savvy managers

   D. Resentful customers

5. Which of the following is least likely to cause a crisis in an organization?

   A. Bribery and corruption

   B. Hostile takeover

   C. Rumours and gossiping

   D. Sexual harassment

6. A public relations disaster can be prevented by

A. Crisis prevention through foresight

B. Crisis prevention through hindsight

C. Having a larger marketing budgets

D. Preparing a better business plan

7. Which event is least likely to be part of a large publishing firm's contingency plan?

A. Absenteeism issues

B. Copyright infringements

C. Information sabotage

D. Product recalls

8. Which of the following is not a potential drawback of contingency planning?

A. Contingency planning can be expensive

B. Some risks are not quantifiable, thereby making planning difficult

C. The incident planned for is less likely to occur over time

D. The incident planned for might not ever happen

9. Quantifiable risks are those that are

A. Difficult or impossible to measure

B. Expensive to insure against

C. Financially measurable threats

D. Natural in occurrence

10. Which of the following is most likely to be an unquantifiable risk for a cinema?

A. A natural disaster that destroys the cinema

B. Assault from customers

C. Copyright infringements

D. Loss of valuable stock

